C000303448

THE EVERYDAY
Low-FODMAP
COOKBOOK

THE EVERYDAY
Low-FODMAP
COOKBOOK

*Easy Recipes to Soothe Inflammation
and Reduce Discomfort*

Zorah Booley, CREATOR OF IN THE MIDNIGHT KITCHEN

PAGE STREET
PUBLISHING CO.

PAGE STREET
PUBLISHING CO.

Copyright © 2021 Zorah Booley

First published in 2021 by
Page Street Publishing Co.
27 Congress Street, Suite 105
Salem, MA 01970
www.pagestreetpublishing.com

All rights reserved. No part of this book may be reproduced or used, in any form
or by any means, electronic or mechanical, without prior permission in writing
from the publisher.

Distributed by Macmillan, sales in Canada by The Canadian Manda Group.

25 24 23 22 21   1 2 3 4 5

ISBN-13: 978-1-64567-279-1
ISBN-10: 1-64567-279-4

Library of Congress Control Number: 2020948581

Cover and book design by Rosie Stewart for Page Street Publishing Co.
Food styling by Zorah Booley
Photography by Junaid Samaai

Printed and bound in China

Page Street Publishing protects our planet by donating to nonprofits like
The Trustees, which focuses on local land conservation.

To anyone who has ever felt restricted by their diet.

To those who love eating out but know the menu can be limited.

To our bodies that endure so much and yet show up every day to be better for us.

To making the necessary lifestyle changes to be able to show up for those who count on us the most.

We do amazing things every day for everyone around us, and it's about time we choose ourselves and take a stand for the way we want to live. I hope these recipes bring comfort into your home and light into your life.

All my love,

Zorah

TABLE OF
Contents

Introduction: Making Sense of Your Gut Through Healthy Eating

We live in a fast-paced world where we all are constantly on the go, and by the end of the day we often ask ourselves, "Where did the time go?" Truth be told, we have no time—especially not for bloating, gas, constipation and cramps. For some of us, however, the reality is that they're here and cannot be ignored. Instead, we have to adapt.

About six years ago I was happily enjoying an eggs Benedict, my standard breakfast order at a new up-and-coming bistro. However (a big however), twenty minutes after the meal, I felt my stomach tossing and turning as if I had food poisoning. The cramps came and so did the pain, and that essentially put the rest of my morning and afternoon on hold. This unusual reaction to a seemingly standard breakfast encouraged me to do some research, and I discovered that I might have developed an allergy to eggs and cow's milk. A visit with the doctor confirmed it. And then came a Truth Bomb: "You have IBS and should start on a low-FODMAP diet."

Then there was a time when the celery juice craze was going viral and I, for one, needed to hop on that bandwagon (even if only for the sake of social media). Very soon after, I realized that I am not like everyone else, in that I can't simply try whatever I please without consequences. In fact, the consequences of me hopping on a seemingly healthy bandwagon included multiple bathroom visits coupled with major physiological discomfort. The thing is, I knew I had irritable bowel syndrome (IBS), but remained optimistic about trying certain health regimens, believing I would be okay. I was sorely mistaken. Yours truly was living in denial about my condition, and a part of me just felt like I was getting older and my body needed a bit more time to adjust.

But surprise! It wasn't about my age or a simple aversion to celery. It was that I wasn't taking into consideration what my body needed: for me to slow down and take stock of how I was feeling after each and every meal. I couldn't just eat everything they served at restaurants or go to dinner at a friend's house and pretend that chickpeas wouldn't make me want to curl into the fetal position and pass out. This presented quite a challenge—and to this day, it still can.

Having had the opportunity to study under talented chefs at Le Cordon Bleu in London, I could not stand the thought of removing anything from my diet, because I really do LOVE food! I was angry at my body for not being able to do what I told it to. I was in denial and felt that my doctor was wrong. And most of all, I was disappointed in myself for not being as strong as I thought I was. After this phase (which lasted a few months), though, I got my act together and started monitoring what I ate every single day. I still do. It's tedious, I'll tell you that much, but I was determined to understand my body and what it needed to create a *new normal*.

What I found out while writing this book is that each person's gut health is unique to them. But there are many ways to incorporate calming, healing ingredients into your cooking and still make every meal enjoyable for you and those who share it with you. One misconception about the low-FODMAP lifestyle is that it's only for those with IBS. This is 100 percent NOT true. Every recipe I've curated here is designed to be enjoyed by everyone in your life, to make a feast for those you care about the most and celebrate food in its most natural and wholesome way. Whether you have IBS or not, you can savor every single one of these recipes.

Having suffered from IBS for six years, I created these recipes for you (yes, you!) to open to any page and think, "Wow! I can eat everything in this recipe and feel pretty darn good afterward." You don't need to feel restricted or as if you have to change your entire way of eating; it's about small adaptations that lead to a healthy, enjoyable lifestyle. That is why I love this book so much. Every chapter, from breakfasts to baked goods, uses ingredients you either have at home or can easily source, and there are no limitations. These recipes are all about eating the way you like and feeling amazing afterward!

Because I'm a chef and a food blogger by trade, I've made this cookbook a love letter from me to you. I'm here to tell you that you no longer have to limit yourself and can live life to the fullest. Everything in moderation can be enjoyed in abundance.

As I always say on my blog, I hope you love Every. Single. Recipe!

Bon appétit,

Zorah

Slow Morning Breakfasts

IT GOES WITHOUT SAYING THAT *breakfast really is the most important meal of the day. Having quick, easy and, most of all, delicious foods for breakfast starts my day on a positive note and gives me the energy I need to tackle what's coming. This chapter pushes some boundaries in the kitchen, letting you embrace your creative spirit. All the ingredients make for a welcoming day ahead— one where you feel comfortable and empowered after you've eaten with no worry of bloating or cramps. There are some gorgeous simple breakfasts, like One-Pot Banana Bread Overnight Oats (page 29), Easy Buckwheat Porridge with Blueberry Compote (page 22) and The Quintessential Green Smoothie with Fresh Kiwi (page 33). And then there are some baked breakfast foods, like Citrus French Toast Casserole (page 17) and Silky Vegan Crepes with Cashew Crème (page 18) that you need for those self-care (Sun)days.*

Pancakes remind me of weekend mornings as a kid, when I would make a batter from just flour, eggs and milk and enjoy my simple pancakes as if I had made a gourmet breakfast. Fast forward a few years (more like two decades) and these blueberry ricotta pancakes may just be my most gourmet pancake ever. The buttermilk and ricotta create a creamy consistency, which really brings through the fluffiness and moist texture in the pancakes. Worried about the dairy here? Don't be! The amounts used in this recipe make it safe for you, allowing you to fully enjoy the flavors.

Oh So Fluffy Blueberry and Ricotta Pancakes

YIELD: 8 TO 10 PANCAKES

In a blender, combine your egg, butter, brown sugar, baking powder, flour, milk and buttermilk and blitz until smooth, 1 to 2 minutes. If you do not have a blender, whisk together the wet ingredients first in a large bowl. Combine the dry ingredients in a separate large bowl, then pour the wet into the dry and whisk until smooth.

At this point, stir in your ricotta cheese, making sure you separate it with your hands to avoid adding it all at once. Stir gently and only for a few seconds.

In a medium frying pan or skillet, set the heat to medium and add 1 tablespoon (14 g) of butter. When the butter starts to sizzle, add ¼ cup (60 ml) of the pancake batter and top the batter with a couple of blueberries. I add my blueberries this way so they don't get mushy, and it also allows me to evenly distribute them among all the pancakes.

After 1 to 3 minutes on low to medium heat, you'll notice bubbles forming. At this point, flip the pancake over and cook the other side for about 1 minute. Repeat until you've used up all the batter. Serve hot garnished with additional ricotta and blueberries.

1 egg

1 tbsp (15 ml) melted butter

2 tbsp + 2 tsp (40 g) brown sugar

1 tbsp (15 g) baking powder

1½ cups (180 g) all-purpose flour

¾ cup (180 ml) milk

½ cup (120 ml) buttermilk

½ cup (120 g) ricotta cheese, plus more for serving

Butter, for the skillet

½ cup (70 g) fresh blueberries, plus more for serving

The Dutch baby originated in Germany (somewhere along the line the name got a bit mixed up) and is essentially a baked, fluffy pancake made in a skillet. As the pancake bakes, it really shows off by puffing up, but after about 2 minutes out of the oven, it slowly deflates, leaving you with an almost cake-like pancake to dive into. This recipe is so easy to follow, and the best part is that all the preparation is done in your blender. It's my no-mess, no-fuss breakfast. And it uses really simple ingredients that your body will appreciate and love you for.

Golden Dutch Baby with Fresh Berries and Mascarpone

YIELD: 3 SERVINGS

Preheat your oven to 450°F (230°C).

Place a medium oven-safe skillet in the oven for 10 minutes until it's hot. Remove the skillet using oven mitts and add half of the butter. Place the skillet back into the oven for another 5 minutes and allow the butter to turn a light golden brown.

While the skillet is heating up, make your batter so that it's ready when the skillet is. In a blender, combine the eggs, milk, flour, brown sugar, cinnamon and the rest of the butter and blitz for 1 to 2 minutes. When your batter is smooth and the butter has browned in the hot skillet, pour the batter into the skillet. Place the berries on top of the batter, spread them out evenly, and pop the pan into the oven to bake for 20 to 25 minutes. Do not open the oven for the first 15 minutes, even if you think the Dutch baby is browning too much, as this will deflate the whole pancake.

When your Dutch baby is ready, remove it from the oven, and top it with the extra berries (if using), maple syrup, confectioners' sugar and mascarpone. The Dutch baby will naturally deflate a bit, but the texture and fullness will remain.

5 tbsp (75 ml) butter, melted, divided

4 eggs

1 cup (240 ml) whole milk

1 cup (125 g) all-purpose flour

1 tbsp + 2 tsp (25 g) brown sugar

1½ tsp (4 g) ground cinnamon

⅓ cup (50 g) fresh blueberries

⅓ cup (40 g) fresh raspberries

Extra berries, for serving (optional)

2 tbsp (30 ml) maple syrup

¼ cup (30 g) sifted confectioners' sugar

1 to 2 tbsp (28 to 56 g) mascarpone, for garnish

This is the queen of French toast right here. The ground cinnamon aids in soothing your gut while the maple syrup is a refined sugar–free sweetener. Plus, this French toast is baked, making it healthier than the traditional recipe. This ticks all the boxes, and I love having some friends over for breakfast so we can all enjoy this casserole together. French toast has always been a treat for me, and once I finally take that first bite, my body automatically thanks me for treating it to some wholesome, homemade food.

Citrus French Toast Casserole

YIELD: 3 TO 5 SERVINGS

Preheat your oven to 400°F (200°C). Move the oven rack to the middle.

In a large bowl, combine your eggs, milk, orange zest and juice, lemon zest and juice, maple syrup, cinnamon, cardamom and nutmeg. Whisk well to incorporate everything together.

Arrange your slices of bread in a 7 x 11–inch (18 x 28–cm) casserole dish, creating two rows of bread slices, and then pour the egg mixture over the bread. Using a pastry brush, brush the melted butter on any slices that are still exposed. Then sprinkle with the brown sugar to get a nice crust. Place the casserole in the oven and bake it for 20 to 30 minutes. When the slices at the top begin to turn a golden brown, you can remove the casserole and enjoy it warm garnished with the lemon zest.

4 eggs

2½ cups (600 ml) whole milk

Zest and juice of 4 oranges

Zest and juice of 1 lemon

¼ cup (60 ml) maple syrup

1½ tsp (4 g) ground cinnamon

1½ tsp (3 g) ground cardamom

1½ tsp (3 g) ground nutmeg

1 loaf sourdough bread, cut into 10 to 12 slices

2 tbsp + 2 tsp (40 ml) melted butter

2 tbsp (30 g) brown sugar

1 tbsp (6 g) lemon zest, for garnish

Crepes are synonymous with France and the ambiance that comes with it, and this recipe brings a touch of Parisian life to your kitchen. These vegan crepes are so light and fluffy, and honestly, you wouldn't even think they could be vegan. This recipe has very simple, wholesome ingredients that really are the start of a great morning. The decadence comes in when you add the cashew crème. While it's not as stiff as if you whipped dairy cream, the nutty flavor pairs with the crepes in the best way. And best of all, no dairy means fewer cramps and aches.

Silky Vegan Crepes with Cashew Crème

YIELD: 8 TO 10 CREPES

Make the cashew crème first. Boil 1⅓ cups (320 ml) of water in a medium pot and add in your cashews. Allow the cashews to cook and soften over medium-low heat for 10 to 15 minutes. When they are soft, strain out the water and pour clean, cool water over them so they aren't too hot. Drain.

In the blender, combine the cashews, 5 tbsp (75 ml) of filtered water, maple syrup and tapioca starch and blitz until the mixture has thickened, about 5 minutes. Scrape down the sides of the blender after each minute. The cream will be quite warm, so allow it to chill in the fridge for at least 1 hour and up to overnight—it will keep its thickness and will be nice and cool to add on top of your crepes.

To make the crepes, in a blender combine the flour, brown sugar, baking powder, milk, vanilla, cinnamon and 1 tablespoon (15 ml) of coconut oil and blitz until smooth, scraping down the blender halfway through. This should take about 2 minutes. When the mixture is smooth and combined, allow it to rest for 15 minutes, then transfer it to a bowl.

Heat a large pan over medium heat and add 1 tablespoon (15 ml) of coconut oil. When it's hot, add in the batter for your first crepe. I like to use a ladle to scoop up about ¼ cup (60 ml) of the batter. Tilt the pan to spread out the batter, then cook for 1 to 2 minutes. When the top of the crepe forms bubbles, you can flip it over and cook the other side for 1 to 2 minutes. When the crepe is a light, golden brown on both sides, you know it is ready.

Repeat with the remaining batter, adding more coconut oil as needed. When you're ready to serve, fold each crepe in half, add some crème and strawberries to one end of the folded crepe, then fold it once more into a quarter and enjoy.

CASHEW CRÈME

4½ oz (126 g) raw cashews, chopped

2 tbsp (30 ml) maple syrup

1½ tsp (4 g) tapioca starch

CREPES

½ cup (63 g) all-purpose flour

1 tbsp + 1½ tsp (20 g) brown sugar

1½ tsp (7 g) baking powder

1½ cups (360 ml) macadamia milk, or any plant-based milk

2 tsp (10 ml) vanilla extract

1½ tsp (3 g) ground cinnamon

3 tbsp (45 ml) melted coconut oil, divided

When you pull this crisp out of the oven, the house is immediately transformed into an old-world bakery, and the warm berry juices burst out of the crisp. Berries provide amazing antioxidants, and just one scoop of this with a little plain yogurt on top will leave you feeling as if you got all your nutrients for the day. It's topped with a light crisp that contains minimal sugar but just enough to balance the tart berry taste. The best part is that this crisp can keep in the fridge, covered with plastic wrap, for up to 3 days, so your breakfast is ready to go for the week ahead.

Summer Berry Crisp

YIELD: 3 TO 6 SERVINGS

To make the berry mixture, coat the bottom of a 9 x 13–inch (23 x 33–cm) baking dish with the melted butter.

In a medium bowl, combine all your berries, lime zest and juice, brown sugar, cinnamon and star anise and stir with a spatula to combine. Cover the bowl with a tea towel and place it in the fridge while you make your crumble.

Preheat your oven to 350°F (175°C).

To make the crumble, in a medium bowl, add your flour and 2 tablespoons (30 g) of brown sugar, and give it a quick whisk to remove any lumps. Add the butter to your flour mixture and start to crumble the flour, sugar and butter using your fingertips. This should take 5 to 10 minutes. Once the butter parts and the mixture starts to become light and crumbly flakes, you know you're done. The crumble should turn a golden sandy color.

Add your berry mixture to the baking dish and spread it out evenly. Then add your crumble on top by squeezing it in a fist and slowly releasing it on top of your berries. This will create large and smaller pieces scattered over your berries. Sprinkle the last 2 teaspoons (10 g) of brown sugar on top of the crumble (if using) and place the dish in the oven for 20 to 25 minutes.

When the crumble turns golden brown, you can remove it from the oven and add any toppings you want. Remember the crumble is hot, so eat with care.

BERRY MIXTURE

2 tbsp (30 ml) melted butter

1 cup (140 g) fresh blueberries

¾ cup (100 g) fresh raspberries

¾ cup (108 g) fresh blackberries

Zest and juice of 1 lime

½ cup (110 g) brown sugar

2 cinnamon sticks

3 star anise pods

CRUMBLE

1½ cups (200 g) all-purpose flour

2 tbsp (30 g) brown sugar + 2 tsp (10 g) for sprinkling (optional)

⅓ cup + 1 tbsp softened butter, cut into cubes

Buckwheat is a super food that many people aren't aware of. It improves heart health, is used to manage diabetes and is a great source of energy and fiber. I topped this with a quick blueberry compote and toasted coconut flakes to take this simple porridge and turn it into a delicious masterpiece. I love how filling this dish is, and because it releases energy slowly, you won't feel a need to snack throughout your morning.

Easy Buckwheat Porridge with Blueberry Compote

YIELD: 1 TO 2 SERVINGS

Begin by putting your buckwheat groats in a fine-mesh colander and rinsing them twice with tap water. Then, soak the buckwheat in a large pot with 2 cups (480 ml) of water for 15 to 30 minutes. Drain.

While it's soaking, in a small pot, combine your blueberries, lemon zest and juice, brown sugar and 2 tablespoons (30 ml) of water and bring to a simmer on low heat. After 10 minutes, the blueberries should look softer and start to expel their juice. Stir and simmer for another 10 to 15 minutes on medium heat. Try not to stir too often, as the blueberries will break very easily, but make sure they're not sticking to the bottom of the pot. When they are soft and the juices are coming out to create a compote, remove them from the heat and set them aside until you're ready to add the compote to your porridge.

Preheat your oven to 350°F (175°C). Line a small baking pan with parchment paper.

In a small pot, boil 2½ cups (600 ml) of water. Add the boiling water to the pot with the soaked buckwheat. Place the pot over low to medium heat and simmer for 15 to 20 minutes. The buckwheat will absorb the water and become soft. Stir every so often, so it doesn't stick to the bottom of the pot.

While the buckwheat is cooking, place the coconut flakes on the baking pan and toast them in the oven for 5 to 10 minutes. When the edges of the coconut become golden brown, remove them from the oven and set aside.

After 15 to 20 minutes, most of the water from the buckwheat porridge should be absorbed. At this point, add in the cinnamon, nutmeg and maple syrup and stir to combine. When all the water is absorbed (after about 5 minutes more), stir in the milk for a creamy porridge and simmer for another 5 minutes. Stir in the toasted coconut.

Remove from the heat and transfer to bowls. Top with blueberry compote and enjoy warm.

1 cup (150 g) buckwheat groats

1 cup (140 g) fresh blueberries

Zest and juice of 1 lemon

¼ cup + 1 tsp (60 g) brown sugar

⅓ cup (35 g) coconut flakes

1½ tsp (3 g) ground cinnamon

1½ tsp (3 g) ground nutmeg

2 tbsp (30 ml) maple syrup

¼ cup (60 ml) whole milk

Breakfast bars are an amazing on-the-go snack that leave you feeling fuller than you would expect, and this recipe contains amazing ingredients that will satisfy and energize you for the day ahead. Thanks to the vitamins and nutrients found in bananas, coconut oil and chia seeds, your gut will be in tip-top shape, too.

The Perfect Breakfast Bar

YIELD: 16 SQUARES OR 8 BARS

Preheat your oven to 350°F (175°C). Line an 8 x 8–inch (20 x 20–cm) baking pan with parchment paper.

In a large bowl, mash the banana with a fork until there are very few lumps. Then add in the peanut butter, egg, coconut oil, maple syrup and vanilla and mix well using a whisk. Then fold in the oats, baking powder, baking soda, cinnamon, salt and chocolate chips.

Pour the mixture into the baking pan and flatten the top using a spatula. Bake for 18 to 20 minutes, until the edges are golden brown. Allow to cool in the pan for 1 hour and then cut into bars or squares.

1 medium ripe banana, peeled

¼ cup (65 g) peanut butter

1 egg

1 tbsp (15 ml) melted coconut oil

2½ tsp (12 ml) maple syrup

½ tsp vanilla extract

1½ cups (135 g) gluten-free rolled oats

¾ tsp baking powder

¾ tsp baking soda

1½ tsp (3 g) ground cinnamon

½ tsp salt

¼ cup (42 g) chocolate chips

This Chocolate Chip Oatmeal Skillet is a decadent yet gluten-free way to start your day. Gluten-packed grains like wheat, barley and rye are high-FODMAP, so oats are a better breakfast choice. The beauty of this incredible meal is the bananas and blueberries underneath, which give the skillet more volume, taste and texture. The blueberries pop through when baked, and the bananas add that soft and rich flavor in every bite. I love the added chocolate chips to really make it feel like you're eating a big baked cookie for breakfast. Top this with some yogurt or enjoy it just as it is.

Chocolate Chip Oatmeal Skillet

YIELD: 3 TO 4 SERVINGS

Preheat your oven to 375°F (190°C). Place a rack in the middle of the oven.

In a medium pot, boil 1 cup (240 ml) of water and add your oats. Cook the oats on medium heat for 10 to 15 minutes or until most of the water has been absorbed. Add in the milk, maple syrup, cinnamon and half the chocolate chips. Stir well and remove the pot from the heat.

Brush a medium oven-safe skillet with the melted butter. Cut 2 of the bananas into rounds and leave the third aside for now. Scatter the slices in the skillet. Set aside a few blueberries for garnish, and arrange the rest in the skillet with the bananas. Then top the fruit with the cooked oats, evenly coating the whole skillet and covering the fruit. Scatter the remainder of the chocolate chips and blueberries on top. Add the walnuts. Cut the last banana in half lengthwise to create two long halves, and arrange them on top. Place the skillet in the oven and bake for 15 minutes.

When the sides of the oatmeal become brown, remove the skillet from the oven. Allow it to cool down for 5 minutes and then dig in.

2¼ cups (200 g) gluten-free rolled oats

1 cup (240 ml) any plant-based milk

2 tbsp + 2 tsp (40 ml) maple syrup

½ tbsp (4 g) ground cinnamon

5 oz (140 g) chocolate chips, divided

1 tbsp (15 ml) melted butter

3 bananas, peeled

1 cup (150 g) fresh blueberries, divided

2 oz (57 g) chopped walnuts

Banana bread is one of my favorite things to bake, and I thought having it for breakfast would be even better with oats. This recipe is perfect for very early mornings when you have no time to actually prepare breakfast. Make it the night before to ensure that you have a solid meal ready before rushing off for the day. These oats are filled with ingredients that really let your body know you're taking care of it.

One–Pot Banana Bread Overnight Oats

YIELD: 1 TO 2 SERVINGS

In a large bowl, combine the oats, plant milk, yogurt, cinnamon, 2 tablespoons (30 ml) of maple syrup and desiccated coconut. Mix well and set it aside.

In a small bowl, use a fork to mash 2 of the bananas. If there are large bits, that is perfectly fine. Add the mashed banana to your oat mixture and combine. Cover your oats with plastic wrap and refrigerate for at least 3 hours or up to overnight.

Preheat your oven to 350°F (175°C). Line a small baking pan with parchment paper.

Place the coconut flakes on the baking pan and toast them in the oven for 5 to 10 minutes. When the edges of the coconut become golden brown, remove them from the oven and set aside to cool until you're ready to mix them in.

When you're ready to assemble your oats, cut the remaining banana half into rounds and scatter them into a glass jar or a small container with a cover. Then spoon your oats over the banana rounds. Top with more banana if you'd like, plus the toasted coconut flakes and 1 tablespoon (15 ml) of maple syrup. Cover the container and take your grab-and-go breakfast with you.

2¼ cups (200 g) gluten-free rolled oats

1½ + ⅓ cups (440 ml) macadamia milk, or any plant-based milk

2 tbsp + 2 tsp (40 ml) plain Greek yogurt

2 tsp (5 g) ground cinnamon

2 tbsp (30 ml) maple syrup + 1 tbsp (15 ml) for topping

⅓ cup (30 g) desiccated coconut

2 bananas + ½ banana for garnish

⅓ cup (30 g) coconut flakes

These overnight groats are one of the most refreshing meals you can have for breakfast. They have a lovely, light crunch to them and a superb creamy consistency. Having this super food blend for breakfast will kick-start your day and leave you feeling satisfied and bloat-free for the rest of the morning.

Carrot Cake Overnight Groats

YIELD: 1 TO 2 SERVINGS

Begin by putting your buckwheat groats in a fine-mesh colander and rinsing them twice with tap water. Then soak the buckwheat in a large bowl with 2 cups (480 ml) of water for 15 to 30 minutes. Drain.

In a medium pot, boil 2¾ cups (660 ml) of water. Add the drained buckwheat to the boiling water. Place the pot over low to medium heat and simmer for 15 to 25 minutes. The buckwheat will absorb the water and become soft. Stir every so often, so it doesn't stick to the bottom of the pot. When most of the water has been absorbed, remove the pot from the heat.

Stir in the milk, carrots, maple syrup, cinnamon, nutmeg, pecans and ⅓ cup (80 ml) of yogurt. Stir well and then cover with plastic wrap and place in the fridge for 3 hours or up to overnight. When you're ready to eat, top with 2 tablespoons (30 ml) of yogurt.

1 cup (150 g) buckwheat groats

1¾ cups (420 ml) whole milk

2 carrots, grated

2 tbsp + 2 tsp (40 ml) maple syrup

2½ tsp (6 g) ground cinnamon

1½ tsp (4 g) ground nutmeg

¼ cup (30 g) chopped pecans

⅓ cup (80 ml) plain Greek yogurt + 2 tbsp (30 ml) for topping

Some days I get so caught up in photo editing and shooting that I forget about breakfast. So before I die of hunger, I always jump to this smoothie to save myself. It's packed with healthy ingredients and nutrients that our bodies crave, including iron, vitamin E, potassium and antioxidants. Natural produce such as spinach and zucchini are vital to keeping us alert and feeling good from the inside out. The added oats help maintain a sense of fullness for hours and really stave off hunger pangs. This smoothie makes 1¾ cups (420 ml), so whether or not there's enough to share depends on how hungry you are.

The Quintessential Green Smoothie with Fresh Kiwi

YIELD: 1 TO 2 SERVINGS

Peel your kiwis and banana and cut the zucchini in half. Place all the ingredients in a blender and blend for 2 to 3 minutes. When the mixture is smooth, pour it into a glass and enjoy.

2 ripe kiwis

1 frozen banana

1½ oz (42 g) baby zucchini

⅓ cup (20 g) chopped baby spinach

1 tbsp (15 g) almond butter

1 cup (240 ml) macadamia milk, or any plant-based milk

2 tbsp (20 g) gluten-free rolled oats

1 tbsp (15 ml) maple syrup (optional)

Easy
Midday
Meals

COMING HOME FROM SCHOOL *as a kid around lunch time, I was always famished. So as I got older, I started making my own lunch. What I made depended on my craving at the moment. To be honest, not much has changed—except now I need wholesome, fuss-free options that help maintain good gut health.*

You might be pleasantly surprised by a few of the recipes in this chapter, like the Authentic Thai Green Curry (page 45) or the Comforting Southern Chili with a Spicy Kick (page 37). It's easy to assume that spicy food leads to discomfort, but that's not the case in these recipes. They have some heat, but not enough to cause an IBS flare-up. I also use Wholesome Homemade Garlic Oil (page 125) as a replacement for whole garlic, because that can be a trigger. It's an easy swap and the results are just as tasty.

Chili is a lunch classic. It's got all the spices and gorgeous smells that make me so happy. This recipe is a bit different than most, because I added some Indian spices to give it an amazing kick, as well as some chicken broth to really plump up the whole meal. And of course, there are no beans. The lovely thing about this recipe is that it's easy to follow, quick to make and, once the simmering is done, you have a pot full of delicious food waiting for you.

Comforting Southern Chili with a Spicy Kick

YIELD: 3 TO 5 SERVINGS

In a large pot over medium heat, add in your garlic oil and melt the butter. Then add in your chopped onion and cook, stirring, for 3 minutes. Continue by adding in the chili powder, paprika, coriander, garam masala, turmeric and peppercorns. Mix well and cook for 2 minutes, until the spices become fragrant.

Add the ground beef to the pot and, using a wooden spoon, mix the ground beef into the spices while breaking up the beef. Let the beef simmer on low heat for 5 to 8 minutes. When all the meat is browned and cooked through, add in the salt, tomato paste, tomato sauce and barbecue sauce. Mix well and let it simmer for 5 minutes.

Finally, stir in the chicken broth, diced tomatoes, sriracha and bay leaves. Then turn the heat to low, put the lid on and let it simmer for 10 to 13 minutes. When it is done, it will be very hot, so be careful not to burn yourself. Top with the avocado slices, sour cream and cheese, and enjoy this comforting meal.

2 tsp (10 ml) Wholesome Homemade Garlic Oil (page 125)

1½ tsp (7 g) butter

²/₃ cup (100 g) chopped onion

2 tsp (5 g) chili powder

1½ tsp (3 g) paprika

1½ tsp (3 g) ground coriander

1½ tsp (3 g) garam masala

1 tsp ground turmeric

1 tsp whole peppercorns

1 lb (454 g) ground beef

1 tsp crushed sea salt

2 tsp (11 g) tomato paste

¼ cup (60 ml) tomato sauce

1 tbsp + 1 tsp (20 ml) barbecue sauce

½ cup (120 ml) Gut-Energizing Chicken Broth (page 122)

2½ oz (70 g) canned diced tomatoes

¾ tsp sriracha

2 bay leaves

2 oz (57 g) avocado, sliced

3 tbsp (45 ml) sour cream

3 tbsp (16 g) grated cheddar cheese

Being Indian, I grew up with savory spices and they just became part of who I am today. I wanted to translate a piece of that experience into this quesadilla and bring you a dish packed with amazing flavors. Add the cheese, sour cream and guacamole, and it becomes a wildly gratifying meal.

Cajun–Inspired Steak Quesadillas with Guacamole

YIELD: 2 LARGE QUESADILLAS

To make the guacamole, add the avocado flesh to a medium bowl. Mash the avocado with a fork, then add the tomatoes, cilantro, lemon juice, salt and pepper and mix well. Cover the bowl with plastic wrap and set the guacamole aside until you're ready to serve.

To make the quesadillas, in a medium bowl combine the Cajun spice, salt, black pepper, oregano, thyme and paprika and stir with a spoon to combine. Add your steak to the spice mixture and rub the spices into the meat using your hands. Cover the bowl with clear plastic wrap and let the meat rest in the spices for 15 minutes or up to 2 hours in the fridge.

In a medium pan, add your garlic oil and allow the pan to heat up on a medium-high heat. When the pan is warm, add your steak and cook each side for 3 to 5 minutes, or 6 to 10 minutes total. When the steak turns a darker brown, it is cooked through. Use a slotted spoon to remove the steak from the pan and place it in a small bowl. Cover with foil to keep the meat warm.

Leave the accumulated spices and oil in the pan. Then add the chopped bell peppers and shallots. Cook, stirring, on medium heat until everything is soft, 10 to 13 minutes. Add the steak back to the pan with the bell peppers and shallots just to warm everything up for 2 minutes, then turn off the heat.

Lay out one tortilla on a work surface. On one half of the tortilla, add half the steak and pepper mixture. Top it with half of the cheese and add 1 tablespoon (15 ml) of the sour cream. Fold the tortilla in half. Repeat with the other tortilla.

Heat a large nonstick pan over medium-high heat and add in the olive oil. Place your tortilla in the pan and cook for 1 to 2 minutes on each side. When both sides are crispy and golden brown, remove from the pan and cut the tortilla in half, exposing the filling. Repeat with the other tortilla, adding more oil if necessary.

When you're ready to eat, top each quesadilla with 1 tablespoon (15 ml) of the sour cream and 1 tablespoon (14 g) of the guacamole and enjoy!

GUACAMOLE

2 avocados, peeled and pitted

1 oz (28 g) chopped tomatoes

2 tbsp (2 g) chopped fresh cilantro

1 tbsp + 1 tsp (20 ml) lemon juice

½ tsp coarse salt

1½ tsp (3 g) black pepper

QUESADILLAS

1½ tsp (3 g) Cajun spice blend

½ tsp coarse salt

1 tsp black pepper

1 tsp dried oregano

1½ tsp (2 g) dried thyme

1½ tsp (3 g) paprika

13 oz (364 g) beef steak, cubed

1 tbsp + 1 tsp (20 ml) Wholesome Homemade Garlic Oil (page 125)

2 oz (57 g) diced yellow bell peppers

2 oz (57 g) diced red bell peppers

2 oz (57 g) diced shallots

2 (7- to 12-inch [18- to 30-cm]) flour tortillas

2 oz (57 g) shredded Manchego cheese

⅓ cup + 2 tbsp (110 ml) sour cream, divided

2 tsp (10 ml) extra-virgin olive oil

2 tbsp (28 g) guacamole

Cooking risotto used to be such a daunting task for me. I was always afraid of making it too dry or too mushy. But after testing different methods, I found that patience is the most important element! This risotto is packed with great flavors and is made with a homemade chicken broth that creates a lovely, hearty meal with the earthy scent of mushrooms wafting through every so often. The chicken broth, combined with the soft spices, helps to create a healthy environment for your gut.

Balsamic Mushroom Risotto

YIELD: 3 TO 5 SERVINGS

In a large pot, warm the garlic oil and butter on medium heat. When the butter begins to sizzle, add in the shallots and cook until they become translucent, 3 to 5 minutes. Add in the oregano, Cajun spice, basil, coriander and paprika and stir well. After about 3 minutes, the spices should bloom and smell fragrant. Add in the mushrooms and sauté for 5 to 8 minutes on low heat.

Add in the arborio rice and stir so it is well mixed with the spices and herbs, then add in the teriyaki sauce and vinegar. Turn the heat back up to medium and add 1½ cup (240 ml) of the warm chicken broth at a time. Stir the rice almost continuously so that it absorbs the liquid faster, and only add in the next cup when all the broth from the previous cup has been absorbed. If you would like your rice even softer, continue to add ½ cup (120 ml) of broth at a time until you've reached the desired consistency.

When all the broth is absorbed, add the grated cheese and parsley, reduce the heat to low, and cook for 5 minutes. The rice should be soft and tender, with some broth still remaining at the bottom of the pot to avoid burning. Season with salt before serving.

2 tbsp (30 ml) Wholesome Homemade Garlic Oil (page 125)

1 tbsp (14 g) butter

5 tbsp (50 g) chopped shallots

1 tbsp (5 g) dried oregano

1½ tsp (3 g) Cajun spice blend

1 tbsp (5 g) dried basil

2½ tsp (4 g) ground coriander

1 tbsp + 1 tsp (9 g) paprika

2½ oz (70 g) porcini mushrooms, roughly chopped

2½ oz (70 g) white mushrooms, roughly chopped

1½ cups (240 g) arborio rice

1 tbsp + 1 tsp (20 ml) teriyaki sauce

2 tbsp (30 ml) balsamic vinegar

2 ⅓ cups (560 ml) Gut-Energizing Chicken Broth (page 122), warmed

3 oz (84 g) Parmesan cheese, grated

¼ cup (15 g) chopped fresh Italian parsley

Salt

This has become a weekly standard in my household. Shrimp is a great addition to your gut-healthy lifestyle, and it contains plenty of protein to keep you full throughout the day. For the sweet chili sauce, I like the one from Trader Joe's.

Spicy Shrimp with Egg Fried Rice
YIELD: 2 TO 4 SERVINGS

Day-old rice is the best choice for this dish, and if you're using it, you can skip to the next paragraph. Otherwise, cook the rice first. Take your uncooked rice and rinse it three times under running water, then drain it. Add the rice to a medium pot and add in 1¾ cups (420 ml) of boiling water and the salt, and set the heat to medium. When the water has been absorbed and the rice is fully cooked (this should take 10 to 15 minutes), pour the rice into a colander to let any excess water drain out. Put the rice back in the pot, add the butter on top, set the heat to very low, and cover with the lid. This allows the rice to steam and firm up before using it. Steam the rice for 7 to 10 minutes.

Clean your shrimp with cold water and pat them dry with a paper towel. Then, using a sharp paring knife, cut down the back of the shrimp and remove the vein. Then cut deeper and open the shrimp up into a butterfly cut. When they are all cut open, pat them dry again and set them aside on a flat plate or tray.

In a small bowl combine the mayonnaise, mustard, sweet chili sauce, cilantro, garlic, chili, lemon juice, salt and black pepper. Using a teaspoon, spoon the mixture onto the shrimp and cover the whole inside of the shrimp with the sauce.

Heat a flat-bottomed pan or a wok over medium heat and add in the garlic oil. Turn the heat up to high and add your shrimp, sauce side down. Press down with a spatula for a few seconds to keep the butterfly shape, and cook for 2 to 3 minutes. Then flip the shrimp and do the same on the other side. The shrimp should look golden brown and a bit charred. When the shrimp are done, start making the fried rice.

In a small bowl, whisk the eggs and add the salt and black pepper.

Heat the wok over medium-high heat. When it's hot, add in the peanut oil. When the oil is warm, add the eggs and stir constantly with a spatula until the eggs are scrambled. After 3 to 4 minutes, add in the scallions. Toss the cooked rice into the wok, along with the coconut aminos, and keep stirring the mixture every so often for 5 to 10 minutes, until the rice is done and some parts are a bit toasted.

To serve, place the rice in a bowl, top it with the shrimp and garnish it with the cilantro.

RICE

1 cup (186 g) long-grain basmati rice, or 3 cups (195 g) day-old cooked rice

½ tsp salt

1 tsp butter

SHRIMP

16 to 20 raw shrimp, peeled

2 tbsp + 2 tsp (40 ml) mayonnaise

1 tbsp (15 ml) Dijon mustard

1 tbsp (15 ml) sweet chili sauce

5 tbsp (5 g) chopped fresh cilantro

2 tbsp (15 g) grated garlic

½ green chili pepper, finely chopped

2 tsp (10 ml) lemon juice

Pinch of salt

Black pepper

2 tbsp (30 ml) Wholesome Homemade Garlic Oil (page 125)

FRIED RICE

2 eggs

½ tsp salt

1½ tsp (3 g) black pepper

2 tsp (10 ml) peanut oil

⅓ cup (16 g) chopped scallions

1 tbsp (15 ml) coconut aminos

Fresh cilantro, for garnish

When I visited Thailand back in my early twenties, the thing that stood out to me was the cuisine. I fell in love with this recipe after that trip, and since then it's been one of my favorites. This dish is designed to make it easier for your gut to digest and to still feel happy and content. I love the calming flavors of the coconut milk and cardamom, and I'm sure you will come to love it too.

Authentic Thai Green Curry

YIELD: 3 TO 4 SERVINGS

Add the butter and garlic oil to a large pot set over medium heat. Add the diced shallots and sauté until translucent, roughly 10 minutes. Then add in the cloves, cardamom, fennel seeds, coriander, cumin and salt. Stir and let simmer for 3 minutes.

Add the chicken breasts to the pot along with the diced bell peppers. Cook for 10 minutes, stirring every few minutes. Add in the Thai green curry paste and the coconut milk, give it a good stir and reduce the heat to low. Cover the pot with a lid and allow the mixture to simmer for 15 to 20 minutes.

When you're ready to serve, add in the chopped cilantro and revel in a little taste of Thailand.

1 tbsp (14 g) butter

1 tsp Wholesome Homemade Garlic Oil (page 125)

5 tbsp (50 g) diced shallots

4 cloves

3 cardamom pods

1½ tsp (3 g) fennel seeds

1½ tsp (4 g) ground coriander

1½ tsp (4 g) ground cumin

½ tsp salt

2 medium boneless chicken breasts, cut on the diagonal into slivers

¼ cup (40 g) diced red bell pepper

3 tbsp (30 g) diced yellow bell pepper

1½ tsp (8 g) Thai green curry paste

1 cup (240 ml) coconut milk

¼ cup (4 g) chopped fresh cilantro

When fall comes around, so does soup season. This amazing vegetable soup is absolutely delicious, with all the soft vegetables needed to create a healthy gut and a happy tummy. The vegan dumplings are such a treat, and they add some carbs to make you feel a bit more satisfied, so you don't need any bread with the soup.

Vegetable Soup with Vegan Dumplings

YIELD: 5 SERVINGS

Preheat the oven to 425°F (220°C).

Grease a large 14- or 16-inch (35- or 40-cm) roasting dish with half the olive oil, then add the white potato, sweet potato, carrots, celery, butternut squash and leeks to the dish. Toss in the rest of the olive oil, salt, pepper, garlic, thyme and rosemary. Place in the oven and roast for 20 minutes.

Meanwhile, prepare your dumplings. Add the flour, baking powder, salt, pepper, basil and thyme to a medium bowl and whisk to combine. Then add in the olive oil and ⅓ cup (80 ml) of water and stir with a wooden spoon until the dough comes together.

Flour a clean surface with 2 tablespoons (16 g) of flour and knead the dough for 3 minutes. When it comes together, form it into a ball, place it back in the same bowl and cover with a clean tea towel.

When the vegetables are roasted, remove the pan from the oven, then remove and discard the whole garlic and fresh herbs. Place the vegetables in a large pot, add the vegetable stock and, using an immersion blender, blend everything together. You can also place them in a stand blender and blend until smooth, then return the soup to the pot. Add the bay leaves, then set the soup aside for now.

Take the dough mixture for the dumplings and divide it into five equal parts. Then roll each part into five smaller round balls.

Set the heat to the lowest temperature on the stove and place the pot of soup on that burner. Add the dumplings to the soup, spaced evenly apart. Cover the pot with the lid and cook for 20 to 30 minutes on low heat. Then turn the heat off and do not open the lid until you are ready to serve, as the air will deflate the dumplings.

SOUP

⅓ cup (80 ml) olive oil, divided

½ cup (70 g) peeled and diced white potato

½ cup (65 g) peeled and diced sweet potato

⅓ cup (40 g) diced carrots

⅓ cup (30 g) chopped celery

¼ cup (30 g) peeled and cubed butternut squash

3 tbsp (20 g) chopped leeks

½ tsp salt

2 tsp (4 g) black pepper

¼ cup (30 g) whole cloves garlic

5 sprigs fresh thyme

3 sprigs fresh rosemary

2⅓ cups (560 ml) vegetable stock

2 bay leaves

DUMPLINGS

1 cup (125 g) + 2 tbsp (16 g) all-purpose flour + more for kneading

2½ tsp (11 g) baking powder

½ tsp salt

1 tsp black pepper

1 tbsp (3 g) dried basil

1 tbsp (3 g) dried thyme

1½ tsp (8 ml) olive oil

Gnocchi is an Italian pasta/dumpling that's usually made from potatoes. But in this recipe, I decided to use pumpkin instead. Pumpkin is a great soft vegetable that is used a lot in a low-FODMAP diet because it doesn't irritate your gut at all. You'll probably have some left over—store it in an airtight container in the refrigerator (it's great added to smoothies). This recipe showcases the pumpkin flavor in the gnocchi, and the brown butter sauce balances it beautifully.

Brown Butter Pumpkin Gnocchi

YIELD: 2 TO 3 SERVINGS

To make the gnocchi, in a medium pot, bring 2½ cups (600 ml) of water to a boil and add the pumpkin. Boil for 25 minutes. When the pumpkin is soft, strain the water out, allow the pumpkin to cool for 15 minutes, and then put it in a medium bowl and mash it up with a potato masher. Measure out ½ cup (58 g)—try to be exact with your measurement.

In a medium bowl, add the ½ cup (58 g) mashed pumpkin, ricotta cheese, Parmesan cheese, pepper and ½ teaspoon of salt. Use a wooden spoon to mix the ingredients. Then add in the rosemary and flour, and mix again to combine. When the dough starts to come together, flour a clean surface and turn out the dough.

Knead the dough until it forms a nice soft ball that is tacky but still pliable, 5 to 8 minutes. If the dough seems a bit too wet, add 1 teaspoon of flour to make it easier to work with. Roll the dough into a long log to about 1½ inches (4 cm) in diameter. Then, using a sharp knife or a dough scraper, cut your gnocchi into 1-inch (2.5-cm)-long pieces. You can roll them with a fork to get the grooves that are typical of gnocchi (it helps to retain the sauce), but this is not necessary. Make sure to toss the cut gnocchi in flour so they don't stick together.

Boil 3 cups (720 ml) of water in a medium pot. When the water is boiling, add 1 teaspoon of salt and the olive oil, then add in the gnocchi, making sure they're fully submerged in the water. When the gnocchi float to the top (after about 15 minutes), strain and set aside.

To make the brown butter sauce, in a large saucepan combine the oil, butter, sage, rosemary, salt and pepper and allow the butter to bubble. Add in the gnocchi and increase the heat to high. Toss the gnocchi in the sauce for 5 to 7 minutes. Pour in the half and half and cook for another minute.

To serve, place a spoonful of the ricotta cheese at the base of your plate. Spoon the gnocchi and some sauce onto the ricotta cheese and season with salt and pepper.

GNOCCHI

1 cup (116 g) peeled and cubed fresh pumpkin

½ cup (123 g) ricotta cheese

¼ cup (25 g) grated Parmesan cheese

1½ tsp (3 g) black pepper

1½ tsp (9 g) salt, divided

1½ tsp (2 g) dried rosemary

1¼ cups (156 g) all-purpose flour + more for dusting

1 tbsp (15 ml) olive oil

BROWN BUTTER SAUCE

2 tbsp (30 ml) olive oil

3 tbsp (42 g) butter

⅓ oz (9 g) fresh sage leaves

2 tbsp (3 g) fresh rosemary

½ tsp salt

1½ tsp (3 g) black pepper

¼ cup (60 ml) half and half

TO SERVE

3 tbsp (50 g) ricotta cheese

Salt

Black pepper

Let's just dive straight into this spicy chicken orzo, because I cannot get enough! This recipe is so comforting and will provide your body with wholesome and nourishing food while also delivering contentment after a long day. This one-pot meal is quick and easy, but so tasty that it will seem as if you've been in the kitchen for hours.

Quick 'n' Spicy Chicken Orzo

YIELD: 2 TO 4 SERVINGS

In a large flat-bottom pan, heat the garlic oil on medium-high heat. Add the chicken pieces to the pan and cook each side for roughly 5 to 6 minutes. When the skin becomes golden brown and crispy, remove the chicken from the pan, place it in a bowl and set it aside.

Lower the heat to medium-low, and in the same pan, add the shallots, cumin seeds, ground cumin, coriander, cinnamon, chili powder, salt and pepper. Sauté the mixture for 3 to 4 minutes, until the spices bloom and become fragrant. Then add in the orzo and stir to combine everything. Turn the heat up to medium-high and cook for 5 to 6 minutes, stirring, then add in the chicken and mix well. Add the diced tomatoes and chicken broth and raise the heat to high. Bring the mixture to a boil for 5 to 8 minutes. You'll know when the liquid is at the right temperature when there are sporadic bubbles popping up. Then add in the coconut milk and stir well.

Turn the heat to low, cover your pan with a lid and simmer for 20 to 25 minutes. The orzo should be soft. Season to taste with more salt and stir in the cilantro. Before serving, garnish with sliced cherry tomatoes and fresh basil!

1 tbsp (15 ml) Wholesome Homemade Garlic Oil (page 125)

1 whole chicken, cut into pieces, or 4 to 6 chicken pieces, bone-in and skin-on (I use thighs, legs and wings)

½ cup (80 g) chopped shallots

1½ tsp (3 g) cumin seeds

1½ tsp (3 g) ground cumin

1 tsp ground coriander

1½ tsp (3 g) ground cinnamon

1½ tsp (4 g) chili powder

½ tsp salt

1½ tsp (3 g) black pepper

7 oz (196 g) orzo

4½ oz (126 g) canned diced tomatoes

2 cups (480 ml) Gut-Energizing Chicken Broth (page 122)

⅓ cup (80 ml) coconut milk

¼ cup (4 g) chopped fresh cilantro

½ cup (79 g) sliced cherry tomatoes, for garnish

1 cup (20 g) fresh basil, for garnish

Sun-dried tomatoes have the most amazing sweet and savory flavor, and this recipe really elevates them while packing in key nutrients such as iron, potassium and vitamin C. The cheeses, fresh basil, lemon juice and garlic oil round everything out, giving you a delicious meal that comes together in no time.

Creamy Pesto Rosso Linguine

YIELD: 2 TO 4 SERVINGS

To make the pesto, add the sun-dried tomatoes, mascarpone cheese, basil, sugar, garlic oil, Parmesan cheese and lemon juice to a food processor and blend until it's smooth and the color resembles that of salmon. Set aside.

Cook the pasta according to package instructions, adding the salt and oil to the boiling water. When your pasta is ready, drain it but reserve ½ cup (120 ml) of the pasta water. Put the cooked pasta and the reserved water in the pasta pot. Then add in the pesto rosso and stir to combine.

When you are ready to serve, garnish the dish with the sliced sun-dried tomatoes and fresh basil.

PESTO ROSSO

8 oz (224 g) sun-dried tomatoes in oil

2 tbsp (25 g) mascarpone cheese

¼ cup (10 g) chopped fresh basil

1 tbsp (15 g) sugar

1 tbsp + 1 tsp (20 ml) Wholesome Homemade Garlic Oil (page 125)

½ cup (50 g) grated Parmesan cheese + more for garnish

1 tsp lemon juice

PASTA

7 oz (196 g) linguine

1 tsp salt

2 tsp (10 ml) olive oil

GARNISH

⅓ cup (18 g) sun-dried tomatoes, sliced

½ cup (10 g) fresh basil

Salmon is one of the healthiest foods you can eat when you're following a low-FODMAP diet, so I had to create a gorgeous and wholesome salmon burger for you to enjoy! Salmon has so many amazing benefits, including omega-3 fatty acids, loads of vitamin B, which aids in nutrient absorption, as well as plenty of potassium, which helps to regulate blood pressure and water retention. I included a variety of lovely herbs that perfectly complement the rich salmon flavor and a spicy mayo to kick up the flavor.

Must–Make Salmon Burgers

YIELD: 3 TO 4 BURGERS

Mince your salmon finely, or put it in a food processor and blitz until just very small pieces of salmon remain.

In a medium bowl, add the salmon, shallots, parsley, mayonnaise, bread crumbs, eggs, salt, pepper, oregano and paprika. Stir well to combine. Let the mixture sit for about 5 minutes so everything can bind together.

In a large skillet, add the garlic oil and set the heat to medium. Scoop up about 2 tablespoons (35 g) of the salmon mixture and shape it into a patty in the palm of your hand, then add it to the pan. Add about three patties at a time to your skillet. Brown the patties for 5 to 8 minutes, then turn them over, cover the pan with a lid, and cook the other side for 5 to 8 minutes more. Repeat with the remaining salmon mixture.

While the patties are cooking, make the spicy mayo. Put all the ingredients in a small bowl and whisk to combine.

When all the patties are done, sandwich two patties between each bun, add the spicy mayo and top with fresh lettuce and tomato.

SALMON BURGERS

7 oz (196 g) skinless salmon fillets

½ cup (80 g) chopped shallots

1½ tbsp (6 g) chopped fresh parsley

1 tbsp + 2 tsp (25 ml) mayonnaise

1½ cups (80 g) panko bread crumbs

2 eggs

½ tsp salt

1½ tsp (3 g) black pepper

1 tsp dried oregano

1½ tsp (3 g) paprika

1 tbsp + 2 tsp (25 ml) Wholesome Homemade Garlic Oil (page 125)

SPICY MAYO

⅓ cup + 1 tbsp (95 ml) mayonnaise

2 tbsp + 2 tsp (40 ml) sriracha

2 tsp (10 ml) lemon juice

1½ tsp (3 g) black pepper

TO SERVE

Burger buns

Lettuce leaves

Tomato slices

This one-pot recipe packs in vegetables and protein and lets you spend minimal time in the kitchen making the magic happen. It includes tom yum paste and Asian fish sauce, savory Thai ingredients that are easy to find online. These days, we want quick meals loaded with nutrients that enable us to glow from the inside out. This ramen noodle soup is bursting with so much flavor, and I find it especially calming when I am experiencing an IBS flare-up.

Rich and Warm Ramen Noodle Soup

YIELD: 3 TO 4 SERVINGS

In a large pot, add the butter and garlic oil and set the heat to medium. Add the mushrooms and tomatoes, then stir in the lemongrass, teriyaki sauce, tom yum paste, cayenne pepper, cumin, soy sauce and shrimp. Give everything a good stir and cook for 5 minutes on medium heat.

Add in the chicken broth, lower the heat to a simmer, and add in the ramen noodles, brown sugar and fish sauce. Cover the pot with a lid and cook for 15 minutes on low heat. When the noodles are soft, add in the bok choy and cook for 3 more minutes, then serve.

2 tbsp (28 g) butter

1 tbsp + 1 tsp (20 ml) Wholesome Homemade Garlic Oil (page 125)

2 oz (57 g) white mushrooms, sliced

4 oz (113 g) cherry tomatoes, cut in half

1 stalk fresh or dried lemongrass, cut in half lengthwise, or zest of 1 lemon

1 tbsp (15 ml) teriyaki sauce

1 tsp tom yum paste

1½ tsp (3 g) cayenne pepper

1 tsp ground cumin

2½ tsp (12 ml) dark soy sauce

5 oz (140 g) peeled and cooked shrimp

2⅓ cups (560 ml) Gut-Energizing Chicken Broth (page 122)

7 oz (196 g) ramen egg noodles

1 tsp brown sugar

2 tsp (10 ml) Asian fish sauce

3 stalks bok choy, whole or cut in half lengthwise

We all have those days when the thought of having to make a meal is so daunting because we're exhausted. I feel you! One day I told my husband I was making grilled cheese, and he merely shrugged, obviously not expecting much. But let me tell you, this has got to be the best grilled cheese sandwich I have ever made. The three different types of cheese, with their natural oils, manage to create that ideal gooey stickiness, and the garlic oil and butter crisp up the sourdough bread to absolute perfection. After I eat this sandwich, I am so content, and best of all, my tummy is happy too.

The Grilled Cheese Trifecta

YIELD: 1 SERVING

Spread the Cheddar cheese on one slice of the bread. Then add the tomato slices (if using) on top, along with the thyme. Then add the Manchego and Parmesan cheeses and top with the remaining slice of bread. Spread the butter on the slice of bread facing up.

Heat a small griddle or pan on medium-high heat and add the garlic oil. When the pan is warmed up, add the sandwich with the buttered side facing down. Use a spatula to press down on the bread for 10 seconds, then cook for 5 minutes. Flip the sandwich, pressing down the other side, and cook for 5 minutes more. When all the cheese is melted and the bread is golden brown and crispy, it's ready.

¼ cup (28 g) sliced or shredded Cheddar cheese

2 slices sourdough bread, or your choice of bread

2 slices tomato (optional)

2 tbsp (4 g) fresh thyme leaves

3 tbsp (20 g) shredded Manchego cheese

3 tbsp (20 g) shredded Parmesan cheese

1 tbsp (14 g) butter, at room temperature

2 tbsp (30 ml) Wholesome Homemade Garlic Oil (page 125)

I must admit that on days when my IBS is acting up, all I want to do is cozy up to a warm bowl of chicken soup that can calm and soothe my discomfort. This recipe was created just for that purpose, and it reminds me of a peaceful fall evening with yellow and orange leaves falling from the trees. This is such a great meal to serve the family after a chilly day.

Cozy, Creamy Chicken Soup

YIELD: 5 TO 6 SERVINGS

In a medium pan, heat up 1 tablespoon (14 g) of butter over medium-low heat. Put the chicken in the pan and set the temperature to medium. Cook it on all sides for 5 to 7 minutes, until the chicken is golden brown. Remove it from the pan and set it aside.

In a large pot, add the garlic oil and 1 tablespoon (14 g) of butter and melt it over low heat. Then add in the shallots and cook for 5 minutes. Add in the cumin seeds, ground cumin, turmeric, thyme, coriander, paprika and flour and give it all a good stir. Then add in the chicken and mix well to coat.

Add the chopped tomatoes, celery, carrots and potatoes to the pot, mix everything together and leave the heat on low. Sauté for 3 or 4 minutes, then add in the canned tomatoes, bay leaves, salt and chicken broth. Give everything a good stir and put the lid on the pot. Simmer the soup on low for 25 minutes.

When the soup is ready, turn the heat off, then remove the chicken, thyme and bay leaves. Put the chicken on a cutting board and pull it apart using a knife and fork—the chicken should easily come apart. Using an immersion blender, blend the soup in the pot until smooth. Then add in the cream and put the chicken back in. Reheat the soup for 5 minutes and serve warm.

2 tbsp (28 g) butter, divided

2 boneless, skinless chicken breasts

1 tbsp + 1 tsp (20 ml) Wholesome Homemade Garlic Oil (page 125)

5 tbsp (50 g) chopped shallots

1½ tsp (3 g) cumin seeds

1½ tsp (4 g) ground cumin

1½ tsp (3 g) ground turmeric

2 sprigs fresh thyme

1½ tsp (4 g) ground coriander

1 tbsp (6 g) paprika

1 tbsp (8 g) all-purpose flour

¼ cup (30 g) chopped tomatoes

⅔ cup (70 g) chopped celery

⅓ cup (40 g) chopped carrots

⅓ cup (50 g) diced white potatoes

2½ oz (70 g) canned tomatoes

2 bay leaves

½ tsp salt

4 cups (960 ml) Gut-Energizing Chicken Broth (page 122)

¼ cup (60 ml) cream or half and half

Calming Down for Dinner Time

WHEN WE COOK DINNER, *it's usually after a full day of working and socializing. These recipes are designed to bring you some tranquility and create a healthy space for you without having to worry about the repercussions of the meal you just ate. Being mindful of what you eat and how you feel will reduce the discomfort that may come from eating triggering foods. This chapter has amazing meals that will keep your mind and body safe. These recipes are a combination of cozy comfort food, spicy and interesting dishes and, of course, some classics that we all know and love.*

Dinner is so special because you get to sit down with those you love and talk about your thoughts and feelings; it's a space and time to decompress. I want this chapter to bring those feelings of calm, joy and stillness with every recipe.

Is there anything better than getting your hands sticky while completely devouring some hearty ribs? I think not, dear friends. I have always been a fan of ribs, and I know you are going to just love this recipe as much as I do. It uses easy-to-find ingredients—you probably have most of them in your pantry right now—and it can be paired with any side dish, such as Thyme-Infused Mushroom Ragù (page 113) or Stuffed Acorn Squash with Brown Rice and Chutney (page 118). Get your hands dirty and dig in!

The Best Ever Sticky Barbecue Ribs

YIELD: 2 TO 3 SERVINGS

Preheat the oven to 325°F (160°C). Line a baking sheet with foil and drizzle it with 3 tablespoons (45 ml) of olive oil.

Add the remaining 3 tablespoons (45 ml) of olive oil, the paprika, garlic powder, cumin, thyme, coriander, brown sugar, black pepper and barbecue seasoning to a small bowl and whisk to combine. Place the ribs on the baking sheet and rub the seasoning all over them. Arrange the ribs on the baking sheet with space between them, cover the sheet with another piece of foil and roast them for 40 minutes.

In the meantime, make your sauce. Combine the tomato sauce, soy sauce, teriyaki sauce, honey and balsamic vinegar in a small bowl. Then pour the sauce into a medium pan over medium heat. Bring to a simmer, turn the heat down to low and simmer for about 7 minutes. When the sauce becomes sticky and thick, turn the heat off and wait for the ribs to be done. Turn the heat to a slow flame.

When the ribs are ready, use a pair of tongs or a fork to dip each rib into the pot of sauce and make sure they are coated evenly. Return the ribs to the baking sheet and increase the oven temperature to 425°F (220°C). Roast the ribs, uncovered, for 15 minutes more, until the sauce glazes them. Remove them from the oven and enjoy hot.

RIBS

6 tbsp (90 ml) olive oil, divided

1 tbsp (6 g) paprika

1 tbsp (8 g) garlic powder

1 tsp ground cumin

1 tbsp (3 g) dried thyme

1½ tsp (3 g) ground coriander

2 tbsp (25 g) brown sugar

1½ tsp (3 g) black pepper

1½ tsp (3 g) barbecue seasoning blend

14 oz (392 g) bone-in beef ribs, trimmed of excess fat

SAUCE

½ cup (120 ml) tomato sauce

2 tbsp (30 ml) soy sauce or coconut aminos

1 tbsp (15 ml) teriyaki sauce

¼ cup + 2 tsp (70 ml) honey

1 tbsp + 1 tsp (20 ml) balsamic vinegar

When it comes to lasagna, it's all about the béchamel sauce and cheese for me. So I took those elements and added them to this chicken veggie bake. The béchamel makes this dish so creamy and perfectly complements the vegetables and chicken. I find that this recipe is a great way to waste less food, as well. I always make it when I have too many leftover vegetables in the fridge, so go ahead and substitute whatever you have on hand.

Easy Chicken Vegetable Bake

YIELD: 3 TO 5 SERVINGS

In a small pan, heat the garlic oil on medium heat. Put the chicken slices in the pan along with ½ cup (120 ml) of water and the barbecue seasoning. Simmer on medium heat until the water has evaporated and the chicken is cooked through. Remove the chicken from the pan and set it aside.

In the same pan where you cooked the chicken, add the butter, mushrooms and pepper. Cook for 5 to 10 minutes and remove them from the pan. Set aside.

Add the butternut squash, zucchini and sweet potato to a steamer basket and steam until soft, about 20 minutes. If you don't have a steamer, place a colander over a pot with water in it. The water should not touch the colander. Set the heat to medium-high, and when steam begins to form, add the vegetables and cover the colander with a lid to steam the veggies.

(Continued)

CHICKEN AND VEGGIES

2 tbsp (30 ml) Wholesome Homemade Garlic Oil (page 125)

3 boneless, skinless chicken breasts, sliced into 2-inch (5-cm) pieces

2 tsp (5 g) barbecue seasoning blend

1 tbsp (14 g) butter

1 cup (70 g) chopped button mushrooms

2 tsp (4 g) black pepper

2 cups (232 g) peeled and cubed butternut squash

1 cup (124 g) peeled and cubed zucchini

1 cup (140 g) peeled and cubed sweet potato

4 to 6 sheets lasagna noodles

Easy Chicken Vegetable Bake (Continued)

While the vegetables are steaming, make the béchamel sauce. Bring the milk to a boil in a medium pot over medium heat. Add in the shallots, celery, bay leaves, thyme and basil. Simmer on medium heat until steam starts to appear, 5 to 8 minutes. When you see the steam, switch off the heat and cover the pot. Allow the flavors to infuse for 15 minutes.

Preheat your oven to 350°F (175°C).

When the milk has been infused, strain out all the solids, put the milk back into the pot and return it to the stove. Set the heat to medium and when the milk starts to heat up, add in the flour, nutmeg, cinnamon and salt, and whisk until there are no lumps. Then whisk in the Cheddar cheese and the mushrooms. After about 7 minutes of cooking and whisking, the sauce should be thick. When it can coat the back of a wooden spoon, it is ready.

In an 8-inch (20-cm) square baking dish, arrange the casserole layer by layer. Line the bottom of the dish with 2 or 3 lasagna sheets, then add half the steamed vegetables, followed by half the chicken. Add another layer of 2 to 3 lasagna sheets, followed by half the béchamel sauce. Top the sauce with the remaining vegetables and then the rest of the chicken. Finish with the rest of the béchamel sauce.

Next, make the topping. In a small bowl, combine the bread crumbs, Cheddar and Parmesan cheeses and rosemary, and sprinkle that over the top layer of béchamel sauce. Bake for 20 to 30 minutes. When the cheese starts to turn golden brown, you know the dish is ready to be eaten and enjoyed.

BÉCHAMEL SAUCE

2 cups (480 ml) whole milk

1 cup (160 g) diced shallots

1 cup (100 g) sliced celery

2 bay leaves

1½ tbsp (5 g) fresh thyme

1 tbsp (4 g) dried basil

⅓ cup + 1 tbsp (50 g) all-purpose flour

1½ tsp (3 g) ground nutmeg

1½ tsp (3 g) ground cinnamon

½ tsp salt

2 cups (226 g) shredded Cheddar cheese

TOPPING

½ cup (55 g) bread crumbs

½ cup (57 g) shredded Cheddar cheese

⅓ cup (33 g) grated Parmesan cheese

2 tbsp (6 g) dried rosemary

Sometimes we just need a good old classic to make us feel like we have everything under control. This recipe requires you to make your own meatballs and sauce, and while this may seem daunting, I find that I love it because I can customize them with my preferred spices and herbs. Plus it gives me peace of mind knowing that I used healthy and natural ingredients for me and my family. This sauce is rich and flavorful, and the best part is that there's a lot of it. This is a true comfort meal and one that I am always up for.

Go–To Spaghetti and Meatballs

YIELD: 3 TO 4 SERVINGS

Start by making the meatballs. In a medium bowl, combine the bread crumbs and buttermilk. Stir and set aside to allow the buttermilk to absorb.

Add the ground beef to a large bowl along with the basil, salt, thyme, paprika, cumin, shallots and mushrooms and combine. Then add in the eggs and the buttermilk mixture. Scoop up a big heaping tablespoon of the mixture per meatball and use your hands to shape them into smooth balls.

Add the olive oil to a large, heavy-bottomed pan over medium heat. Place the meatballs in the pan and cook for 5 to 8 minutes per side so that the meatballs brown all over. Make sure they are cooked inside as well; if they still seem a bit uncooked, leave them in the pan for 5 more minutes on each side. When they are done, remove them from the pan and set aside.

Preheat the oven to 425°F (220°C).

(Continued)

MEATBALLS

⅔ cup (70 g) bread crumbs

¾ cup (180 ml) buttermilk

1 lb (454 g) ground beef

2 tbsp (8 g) dried basil

½ tsp salt

2 tbsp (6 g) dried thyme

1½ tsp (3 g) paprika

1½ tsp (4 g) ground cumin

5 tbsp (50 g) chopped shallots

⅓ cup (18 g) finely chopped white mushrooms

2 eggs

2 tbsp (30 ml) olive oil

Go-To Spaghetti and Meatballs (Continued)

Make the tomato sauce. In a large roasting dish, toss the olive oil, shallots, tomatoes (with accumulated juice), garlic cloves, basil, sugar, salt and peppercorns. Roast for 30 to 40 minutes. When the shallots are slightly charred and the oven is smelling fragrant, remove the dish and transfer the contents to a large pot. Remove and discard the garlic to avoid any IBS flare-ups.

Place the pot over medium heat and add the chicken broth. Allow the sauce to come to a soft boil and cook for 10 minutes. Remove the pot from the heat, then blend the sauce until smooth using an immersion blender or in a blender or food processor. Return the sauce to the pot, add the meatballs and simmer everything on low to medium heat for 15 to 20 minutes. The sauce should get thicker and small bubbles should appear.

While the sauce cooks, make the spaghetti. In a large pot over medium-high heat, bring 2⅓ cups (560 ml) of water to a boil along with the salt and olive oil. When the water starts to boil add in the spaghetti and cook for 10 to 14 minutes, until the pasta is al dente. Drain and divide the pasta evenly among three or four bowls. Top with the sauce and meatballs and sprinkle on the Parmesan cheese.

TOMATO SAUCE

2 tbsp (30 ml) olive oil

¾ cup (130 g) roughly chopped shallots

2 cups (360 g) diced tomatoes

3 whole cloves garlic

¼ cup (10 g) chopped fresh basil

1 tbsp (14 g) brown sugar

½ tsp salt

1½ tsp (3 g) whole peppercorns

¾ cup (180 ml) Gut-Energizing Chicken Broth (page 122)

SPAGHETTI

½ tsp salt

1 tbsp (15 ml) olive oil

10 oz (280 g) spaghetti

¾ cup (75 g) grated Parmesan cheese

This protein-packed dinner is beautifully paired with a light mushroom sauce. I love how creamy the sauce is, and it does not take away from the natural flavor of the beef, which I really appreciate. Cooking beef can be tricky, so I cook it to medium doneness and then remove it from the pan and make the sauce. That way the meat doesn't get overcooked. This is a quick and easy dinner and pairs wonderfully with roasted sweet potato wedges.

Succulent Beef in Creamy Mushroom Sauce

YIELD: 3 TO 4 SERVINGS

In a large skillet, melt the butter on medium-high heat. When it starts to sizzle, add in the beef and sear until both sides are golden brown and slightly darker on the outer edges, 1 to 2 minutes on each side. Remove the beef and set aside. Then lower the heat to low and sprinkle in the flour. When it is all absorbed, add the mushrooms, fresh and dried thyme, oregano and Cajun spice and sauté for 5 to 10 minutes, until everything becomes fragrant.

Add in the chicken broth and turn the heat up to medium. Let the chicken broth thicken for about 5 minutes. Then stir in the cream, cooked beef and Parmesan cheese. Lower the heat and let it simmer for 10 minutes. When it's done, season to taste with salt and pepper.

2 tbsp (28 g) butter

5 to 8 slices beef fillet (10 to 14 oz [280 to 392 g] total)

1 tbsp (8 g) all-purpose flour

1¾ cups (120 g) sliced mushrooms

2 tbsp (4 g) fresh thyme leaves

1 tbsp (3 g) dried thyme

1½ tsp (3 g) dried oregano

2 tsp (4 g) Cajun spice blend

¾ cup (180 ml) Gut-Energizing Chicken Broth (page 122)

¼ cup (60 ml) cream

½ cup (45 g) grated Parmesan cheese

Salt

Black pepper

This is a classic dish that must be ordered when visiting an Indian restaurant—but with this recipe, you can make it at home. I kept this recipe as authentic as possible while also keeping it gut-healthy, and I must say, I nailed it. This curry is a little bit spicy and extremely tasty. I love making this recipe, and it's one that my husband is a fan of, so trust me when I say this is a keeper.

One-Pot Lamb Rogan Josh
YIELD: 2 TO 4 SERVINGS

In a medium bowl, combine the paprika, chili powder, coriander, cumin and garam masala. Cut your lamb into cubes if it's boneless or leave as is if you are using lamb chops, and add them to the bowl of spices. Toss to make sure every piece is coated.

Add the butter and garlic oil to a medium pot over medium heat. When the butter has melted, add in the shallots and cook for 5 minutes, stirring. Then add in the cinnamon, cardamom, cloves, fennel seeds and ginger and stir to combine. When the shallots begin to brown, add in the spiced lamb, tomato purée and the chicken broth. Turn the heat down to low and cover the pot. Simmer on low for 20 minutes, then remove the lid and let it simmer on medium heat for another 10 minutes so the sauce can reduce.

When you're ready to serve, stir in the yogurt and cilantro and serve hot.

1 tbsp (6 g) paprika

1½ tsp (4 g) chili powder

1 tbsp (5 g) ground coriander

1 tbsp (5 g) ground cumin

1½ tsp (3 g) garam masala

11 oz (308 g) lamb chops (with or without bones)

3 tbsp (42 g) butter

¼ cup (60 ml) Wholesome Homemade Garlic Oil (page 125)

½ cup (80 g) diced shallots

1 stick cinnamon

5 green cardamom pods

4 cloves

1 tsp fennel seeds

¾-inch (2-cm) piece fresh ginger, crushed

¼ cup (60 ml) tomato purée

1½ cups (360 ml) Gut-Energizing Chicken Broth (page 122)

¼ cup (60 ml) plain Greek yogurt

¼ cup (5 g) chopped fresh cilantro

For this recipe, I wanted to include a lot of healing ingredients that would both taste amazing and be beneficial for your health. The butternut squash and pumpkin create a very calming environment for the tummy, while the bell peppers add just a little kick. Then the fresh herbs add that X factor to finish things off. I really love this dish, and it just warms my heart when I have a bowl of it because I know my body will thank me later.

Anti-Inflammatory Butternut Pumpkin Soup

YIELD: 3 TO 4 SERVINGS

Preheat the oven to 400°F (200°C).

In a 12-inch (30-cm) roasting dish, drizzle 2 tablespoons (30 ml) of the olive oil, then add the butternut squash, pumpkin, red and yellow peppers, rosemary, thyme, salt, pepper, cloves and cumin seeds. Drizzle with the remaining 2 tablespoons (30 ml) of olive oil and mix everything together.

Roast for 25 minutes, until all the ingredients are soft and slightly browned. After the 25 minutes, remove the cloves and fresh herbs from the roasting dish, place the rest of the ingredients in a blender and blitz until smooth. Transfer the mixture to a medium pot and add in the vegetable stock. Cook the soup on medium heat for 10 minutes. Taste and add more salt, if needed, before serving. Garnish with the croutons, if using.

4 tbsp (60 ml) olive oil, divided

1²/₃ cups (200 g) peeled and cubed butternut squash

1²/₃ cups (200 g) peeled and cubed fresh pumpkin

¼ cup (40 g) roughly chopped red bell pepper

¹/₃ cup (50 g) roughly chopped yellow bell pepper

¼ cup (8 g) fresh rosemary

3 tbsp (8 g) fresh thyme + more for garnish (optional)

½ tsp salt + more to taste

1½ tsp (3 g) black pepper

3 cloves

1½ tsp (3 g) cumin seeds

13 oz (384 ml) vegetable stock

Croutons, for garnish (optional)

When I came up with this recipe, I wanted something similar to sticky coconut rice but with a savory flavor. This risotto combines saltiness with the sweetness you find in the coconut rice. The flavors are just so beautiful when they come together, and the results are so worth the time spent in the kitchen stirring the risotto. This recipe is simple and wholesome, yet feels indulgent.

Coconut Shrimp Risotto

YIELD: 3 TO 4 SERVINGS

Add the butter and garlic oil to a large pot over medium-low heat. When the butter melts, add in the shallots. Cook for 5 minutes, until they're translucent. Then add in the celery seeds, garlic powder, cumin and paprika, and mix well to combine. When they become fragrant, after about 5 minutes, add in the teriyaki and soy sauces. Then add in the rice and stir so that all the rice is coated with the spices and sauces in the pot.

Now raise the heat to medium and add in 1 cup (240 ml) of the warm broth. Cook and stir for about 15 minutes, until all the broth has been absorbed. You want to stir as often as possible or the rice will stick to the bottom of the pot and burn. Then add the next cup and repeat until all the broth has been added and your rice is tender. Make sure the broth has been absorbed before adding the next cup.

When all the broth has been added and absorbed, add in the coconut milk and shrimp and stir, stir, stir for 15 minutes, until the risotto has only a small amount of liquid left. When the risotto is thick and sticky, add in the desiccated coconut and Parmesan cheese and cook, stirring, for 5 minutes more. If the rice becomes too thick, add another ½ cup (120 ml) of warm chicken broth and stir again on medium-high heat until most of the liquid has been absorbed. When you're ready to serve, sprinkle with the flaked coconut and enjoy warm.

1 tbsp (14 g) butter

2 tbsp (30 ml) Wholesome Homemade Garlic Oil (page 125)

⅓ cup (60 g) diced shallots

1½ tsp (3 g) celery seeds

1½ tsp (3 g) garlic powder

1¼ tsp (4 g) ground cumin

1½ tsp (4 g) paprika

1 tbsp (15 ml) teriyaki sauce

1 tbsp (15 ml) dark soy sauce

1¼ cups (240 g) arborio rice

2⅓ cups (560 ml) Gut-Energizing Chicken Broth (page 122), warmed

1 cup (240 ml) coconut milk

8 oz (224 g) peeled, deveined and cooked shrimp

¼ cup (20 g) desiccated coconut

⅔ cup (70 g) grated Parmesan cheese

½ cup (50 g) flaked coconut, for garnish

Khaliya is a chicken curry that originated in Mauritius and has a beautiful blend of spices and a yogurt base. This is a meal I grew up with; at the very least we had it every two weeks. It always reminds me of my mother's cooking. This recipe is filled with gorgeous spices, and a lovely, fluffy bed of basmati rice will bring it all together. When the spices become fragrant, if you are within smelling distance of that kitchen, I know you will be salivating, waiting for this dish to be done.

Back to My Roots Indian Khaliya

YIELD: 3 TO 4 SERVINGS

In a medium pot, bring 2½ cups (600 ml) of water to a boil and add the potatoes. Boil for 15 minutes on high heat. When they are easily pierced with a fork, drain them and set them aside.

In a large pot, heat the butter and oil on medium heat. Add in the coriander, ground cumin, cayenne pepper, cinnamon stick, cumin seeds, garlic powder and ginger. Cook on low heat for 5 minutes until the spices become fragrant. Add in the shallots and cook on medium heat for another 7 minutes, until they are browned. Add the chicken and brown it on both sides, roughly 7 minutes per side. Then add in the tomato paste, diced tomatoes and the potatoes and stir well. Cook for 5 minutes, then add in the chicken broth and give it a good stir.

Add in the curry leaves and salt and turn the heat to low. Let the dish simmer, uncovered, for 20 to 25 minutes. Top with the fresh cilantro just before serving.

4 oz (113 g) white potatoes, peeled and cut into quarters

2 tbsp (28 g) butter

1 tbsp (15 ml) Wholesome Homemade Garlic Oil (page 125)

1½ tsp (4 g) ground coriander

2 tsp (6 g) ground cumin

1½ tsp (3 g) cayenne pepper

1 cinnamon stick

1 tbsp (6 g) cumin seeds

1½ tsp (3 g) garlic powder

¾-inch (2-cm) piece fresh ginger, crushed

5 tbsp (50 g) finely chopped shallots

6 pieces bone-in chicken, with or without skin (ideally legs and breast portions)

1½ tsp (8 g) tomato paste

2½ oz (70 g) diced tomatoes

1⅛ cups (266 ml) Gut-Energizing Chicken Broth (page 122)

3 curry leaves, or 3 bay leaves

½ tsp salt

3 tbsp (3 g) freshly chopped cilantro

I used to dream of duplicating the wonderful sticky sauce you get on ribs and chops in steak houses, and I can finally present to you the best sauce for sticky and sweet lamb chops. This recipe could not be easier to make, and it will have you licking your fingers.

Classic Sticky Maple Lamb Chops

YIELD: 2 SERVINGS

In a medium bowl, combine the barbecue sauce, soy sauce, tomato sauce, sweet chili sauce, maple syrup, balsamic vinegar and brown sugar. Whisk together and transfer the sauce to a medium pot. Bring the sauce to a simmer over medium heat. After 1 to 2 minutes, add in the cornstarch and whisk until there are no lumps. When the sauce begins to boil, remove the pot from the heat and allow the sauce to cool for 5 minutes.

Toss the lamb chops in the pot with the sauce and mix them with a pastry brush or a spatula to make sure all the chops are coated. Cover the pot and place it in the fridge for 1 hour or up to overnight for maximum flavor.

When you're ready to cook, give the chops 30 minutes to come to room temperature. Meanwhile, preheat your oven to 400°F (200°C) and place a rack in the middle of the oven.

Line a baking sheet with foil, shiny side facing up, and arrange the chops on the foil with some space between each one. Roast the chops for 8 to 10 minutes, then flip them and baste with the sauce that's still in the pot. Roast the chops for 8 to 10 minutes more. They should look very glossy and golden brown, and some of the sauce should be slightly darker and sticky. Remove them from the oven and serve warm, garnished with the mint leaves, if using.

3 tbsp (45 ml) barbecue sauce

1 tbsp (15 ml) soy sauce

2 tbsp (30 ml) tomato sauce

1 tbsp + 1 tsp (20 ml) sweet chili sauce

1 tbsp + 1 tsp (20 ml) maple syrup

1 tbsp (15 ml) balsamic vinegar

1 tbsp (14 g) brown sugar

1½ tsp (4 g) cornstarch

4 to 6 lamb chops

½ cup (15 g) mint leaves, for garnish (optional)

We all need a healing soup for those kinds of days when we're sick and congested. Whenever I feel like the flu is on the way, I have to make this soup. It has no noodles or carbs, but the flavor is immeasurable and the spiciness really opens up my senses and leaves me feeling so much better—like I can actually tackle the day ahead without any flare-ups or flu-like symptoms.

Rustic Tom Yum Soup

YIELD: 2 TO 3 SERVINGS

In a large pot, melt the butter over medium heat and add in the chicken broth. Then add in the lemongrass, tom yum paste, fish sauce, brown sugar, teriyaki sauce, kaffir lime leaves, thyme, peppercorns, bay leaves and paprika, if using. Bring the mixture to a boil, then lower the heat and simmer for 10 to 15 minutes, until the ingredients become fragrant.

Add in the mushrooms, tomatoes and shrimp and reduce the heat to low. Simmer for 10 minutes. Finally, add in the coconut milk and cover the pot. Let it simmer again for 5 minutes so the flavors can combine. Serve garnished with the bok choy and scallions—be careful, as it will be very hot!

2 tsp (9 g) butter

2⅓ cups (560 ml) Gut-Energizing Chicken Broth (page 122)

1 stalk lemongrass, fresh or dried

1 tbsp + 2 tsp (25 g) tom yum paste

1 tsp fish sauce

½ tsp brown sugar

1½ tsp (7 ml) teriyaki sauce

5 kaffir lime leaves or fresh lime leaves, or zest of 1 lime

1 tbsp (3 g) dried thyme

1½ tsp (3 g) whole peppercorns

2 bay leaves

1½ tsp (3 g) paprika (optional)

2 cups (120 g) sliced mushrooms

¾ cup (110 g) sliced cherry tomatoes

9 oz (252 g) peeled, deveined and cooked shrimp

⅓ cup + 1 tbsp (95 ml) coconut milk

1 to 2 stalks bok choy, for garnish

¼ cup (26 g) diced scallions, for garnish

This recipe is a layered dish of rice, chicken and potatoes all stirred up in a blend of spices that will delight your taste buds. This Middle Eastern dish is very similar to biryani, which is of Indian origin, but the difference is that with biryani, you strain out the liquid, whereas with pilaf (also known as pilau), the broth and spices are fully absorbed by the rice, making this dish insanely flavorful and delicious. The raita is a topping that adds a cooling element to an otherwise warm dish. What I particularly love about this recipe is that no one would assume it's low-FODMAP, but there's nothing that would trigger your IBS and the spices used don't aggravate the gut at all.

Aromatic Chicken Pilaf

YIELD: 3 TO 4 SERVINGS

Rinse your rice four times, and on the fourth rinse, allow the rice to soak in a bowl of water for 20 minutes, or until you are ready to cook it.

In a large oven-safe pot (or a Dutch oven) over low heat, add in your butter and garlic oil. When the butter has melted, add the shallots to the pot. Turn the heat up to medium and sauté the shallots for 7 to 12 minutes, until they become translucent. Then add in the cinnamon stick, bay leaves, cardamom, cloves, peppercorns, cumin, coriander and ginger. Cook for about 5 minutes, stirring to prevent burning, until the spices become fragrant. Deglaze the pot with 2 tablespoons (30 ml) of water if necessary.

Add the chicken and the potatoes to your pot and cook, stirring occasionally, until the chicken is par-cooked, about 10 minutes on medium heat (the chicken will continue cooking when it goes in the oven). Then add in your tomatoes and dried chilies.

Drain your rice and add it to the pot. Stir, ensuring that all the rice is coated with the sauce, then add in the chicken broth and the salt, stir again and cover the pot with a lid. Simmer on medium heat for 10 minutes.

Preheat your oven to 425°F (220°C). Position a rack in the middle of the oven.

Place the pot, still covered, into the oven and cook the pilaf for 30 to 40 minutes. Do not stir the pot or check the pilaf until it has been at least 30 minutes. The pilaf is done when the rice has absorbed all the water. At this point you can remove it from the oven or leave it to sit in the pot for another 10 minutes. Do not leave it for too long or the chicken could become rather dry.

(Continued)

PILAF

1½ cups (300 g) long-grain jasmine rice

3 tbsp (42 g) butter

1 tbsp + 1 tsp (20 ml) Wholesome Homemade Garlic Oil (page 125)

⅔ cup (120 g) diced shallots

1 cinnamon stick

2 bay leaves

3 green cardamom pods

5 whole cloves

1½ tsp (3 g) whole peppercorns

1½ tsp (3 g) cumin seeds

2 tsp (4 g) ground coriander

1-inch (2.5-cm) piece fresh ginger, crushed

3 boneless, skinless chicken breasts, cut into 1-inch (2.5-cm) strips

2 medium russet potatoes, peeled and cubed

¾ cup (135 g) diced tomatoes

2 dried red chili peppers

1 cup (240 ml) Gut-Energizing Chicken Broth (page 122)

¾ tsp salt

While the pilaf cooks, make the raita. Add the cilantro, mint, yogurt, lemon juice, garlic oil, salt, cumin and black pepper to your blender. Blend until the raita is a light green sage color. This should take 2 to 3 minutes. Scrape down the sides of the blender if some of the yogurt is still sticking to the sides.

When the pilaf is ready, spoon some out onto your plate and drizzle some raita on top to really elevate the dish.

RAITA

¼ cup (4 g) chopped fresh cilantro

1½ tsp (3 g) minced fresh mint

2 cups (480 ml) plain yogurt

1 tsp lemon juice

1 tbsp (15 ml) Wholesome Homemade Garlic Oil (page 125)

½ tsp salt

1½ tsp (4 g) ground cumin

1½ tsp (3 g) black pepper

Brown butter adds so much depth to a dish that it should be in every recipe! This Brown Butter Shrimp is super easy and literally, once you toss in the noodles, it's ready to go. I opted out of adding veggies to make it simpler and easier for those run-around days when we just need a healthy and wholesome meal without much fuss. However, cherry tomatoes and sliced zucchini would be a perfect fit for this recipe if you feel the need for some veg.

Brown Butter Shrimp with Noodles

YIELD: 2 TO 3 SERVINGS

Add the butter to a small pot over medium heat. When it bubbles, add the sage and rosemary, then continue to cook for another 5 minutes to allow the butter to brown. Add the lemon juice and give it a quick stir and remove the pot from the heat. Put the shrimp in the pot with the browned butter and mix well. Remove the sage leaves from the brown butter sauce.

Bring 3 cups (720 ml) of water to a boil in a medium pot. Add the egg noodles and cook for 10 to 15 minutes on medium heat until soft.

While the noodles are cooking, add the peanut oil to a wok or flat-bottomed pan over medium heat. When the oil is warm, add the shrimp and butter sauce and cook for 5 minutes. Then add in the teriyaki sauce and green chili. Sauté for 7 minutes, then add in the coconut milk and bring the mixture to a simmer for another 10 minutes. When the noodles are done, drain them and add them to the wok. Finally, stir in the fresh cilantro and serve.

4 tbsp (56 g) butter

5 fresh sage leaves

1 sprig rosemary

3 tbsp (45 ml) freshly squeezed lemon juice

7 oz (196 g) peeled, deveined and cooked shrimp

2 oz (57 g) egg noodles

2 tbsp (30 ml) peanut oil

3 tbsp (45 ml) teriyaki sauce

½ green chili pepper, chopped

¼ cup (60 ml) coconut milk

½ cup (8 g) chopped fresh cilantro

Risotto is an amazing way to get your greens in. In this recipe, I use darker greens to really boost the potassium, iron and magnesium. I find that balancing carbohydrates, proteins and greens in my daily life really leave me feeling well nourished and content. I don't like to exclude carbohydrates because our bodies need them to burn those calories that give us the energy to get through the day. The Parmesan cheese makes this recipe creamy and the greens add extra flavor and texture.

Healthy All–Green Risotto

YIELD: 3 TO 4 SERVINGS

In a large pot, add the butter and olive oil over medium heat. When the butter has melted, add the onion and cook for 5 to 8 minutes, stirring, until the onion becomes translucent. Add in the peppercorns, cumin, coriander and garlic powder, then stir and sauté for 5 to 10 minutes over medium-low heat. When the spices become fragrant, add in the peas, Swiss chard and fresh basil, and stir. Then add in the rice and mix well, so all the rice is coated. Then add the thyme, dried basil and dried oregano.

Continuing to cook over low to medium heat, add 1 cup (240 ml) at a time of warm vegetable broth while continuously stirring until most or all of the liquid is absorbed. Continue adding the liquid 1 cup (240 ml) at a time until all the broth is added to the rice. Do not add more broth until the broth you added is almost fully absorbed.

When you are done adding all the broth, stir in the chili powder and cheese. The rice should be soft and the risotto should have a little bit of broth (just a few tablespoons) in the bottom of the pot to keep it moist. Spoon the risotto into a shallow bowl, top with extra grated Parmesan and the basil and enjoy warm.

2 tbsp (28 g) butter

2 tbsp (30 ml) olive oil

²/₃ cup (100 g) finely chopped onion

5 whole peppercorns

1 tsp ground cumin

1½ tsp (3 g) ground coriander

1½ tsp (3 g) garlic powder

1 cup (130 g) frozen peas

1 cup (40 g) chopped Swiss chard

¼ cup (10 g) chopped fresh basil

1½ cups (240 g) arborio rice

2 tbsp (4 g) fresh thyme

1½ tsp (2 g) dried basil

1½ tsp (3 g) dried oregano

4 cups (960 ml) vegetable broth or Gut-Energizing Chicken Broth (page 122), warmed

1½ tsp (3 g) chili powder

1 cup (100 g) grated Parmesan cheese + more for garnish

½ cup (10 g) fresh basil, for garnish

Every time I enjoy a bowl of minestrone soup, I'm transported back to Italy. I really wanted this to be a heartwarming dish, just the way I remember it from when I was there. The great thing about this particular soup is that all the vegetables in it are soft fibers, and the variety adds textures and tastes and makes this soup so gorgeous to just look at. I hope you totally enjoy this delicious bowl of warmth and happiness.

Soothing Minestrone Soup

YIELD: 3 TO 4 SERVINGS

In a large pot, heat the garlic oil on low heat, then add in the shallots and sauté for 3 minutes. Add in the ginger, thyme, paprika, cumin, basil and peppercorns. Cook for a minute or two, stirring frequently, then add in the sweet potatoes and russet potatoes.

Allow everything to sweat for 5 minutes and then turn the heat up to medium, pour in ⅓ cup (80 ml) of water to deglaze the pot, and then add in the celery, zucchini, carrots, leeks, butternut squash and ½ teaspoon of salt. Cook for another 5 minutes while stirring.

Add the balsamic vinegar, tomatoes, brown sugar, bay leaves and chicken broth. Reduce the heat to low and cook, stirring every 10 minutes, for 25 minutes.

In the meantime, prepare your macaroni. In a medium pot, bring 3 cups (720 ml) of water to a boil, along with the olive oil and ½ teaspoon of salt. Stir in the macaroni and then cook on medium heat for 15 minutes. When your macaroni is soft but firm, drain and set it aside until you are ready to add it to your soup.

When the vegetables are soft, distribute the soup evenly among bowls, add some of the macaroni to each bowl, and top with shaved Parmesan cheese.

2 tbsp (30 ml) Wholesome Homemade Garlic Oil (page 125)

½ cup + 2 tbsp (100 g) chopped shallots

1 tbsp (5 g) ground ginger

1 tbsp + 1 tsp (4 g) dried thyme

1 tbsp (8 g) paprika

1 tsp ground cumin

2 tbsp (3 g) dried basil

5 whole peppercorns

1 medium sweet potato, peeled and diced into 1-inch (2.5-cm) cubes

1 medium russet potato, peeled and diced into 1-inch (2.5-cm) cubes

1 stalk celery, cut into 1-inch (2.5-cm) slices

3 medium zucchini, peeled and cut into rounds

1 carrot, peeled and diced

2 medium leeks, peeled and cut into rounds

½ cup (55 g) peeled and cubed butternut squash or pumpkin

1 tsp salt, divided

1 tbsp (15 ml) balsamic vinegar

12 oz (340 g) canned peeled and diced tomatoes

2 tsp (10 g) brown sugar

3 bay leaves

3⅓ cups (800 ml) Gut-Energizing Chicken Broth (page 122)

5 oz (140 g) macaroni pasta

2 tbsp (30 ml) olive oil

2 oz (57 g) shaved Parmesan cheese

The spices in this dish really are healing and calming for the gut, and the noodles are just the best way to add some carbs to a meal so that there is no sugar craving an hour later. The kicker for this recipe is the salty fried noodles that get placed on top. They add so much texture and contrast to an otherwise very "soft" dish. This is one of those meals that will become a weeknight special because it's convenient to make and is packed with so much flavor.

Calming Khao Soi with Crispy Noodles

YIELD: 3 TO 4 SERVINGS

Bring a small pot of water to a boil and add 2½ ounces (75 g) of egg noodles. Cook until they're soft, 5 to 10 minutes. Drain the water.

In a medium pot, warm the vegetable oil so it begins to lightly bubble. To check if it's ready, drop a small piece of cooked egg noodle into the pot. It should start to sizzle immediately. Then add in the rest of the cooked noodles and fry for 10 to 15 minutes. When the noodles are golden brown, remove them with a slotted spoon and place them on paper towels so the excess oil can be absorbed. Sprinkle with salt and set the noodles aside.

In a large pot, heat the butter and garlic oil over medium heat. Add the ginger, cumin, cinnamon, paprika, coriander, turmeric and the green chili. Sauté on medium heat for 5 minutes, until fragrant, then add in the cubed chicken. Cook on medium-low heat until the chicken skin is white and you can't see any pink in the chicken, 10 to 15 minutes. Add in the Thai red curry paste and stir to combine everything, then pour in the chicken broth and lime leaves, and simmer for 10 minutes.

In the meantime, bring a medium pot of water to a boil and cook the remaining 1¾ ounces (50 g) of egg noodles for 8 to 12 minutes. The noodles will be soft and tender when they are done. Drain.

When the broth is done simmering, add in the coconut milk, cilantro and the remaining salt. Divide the boiled noodles among individual bowls, pour the khao soi broth on top, and then top with the fried noodles.

4¼ oz (126 g) Chinese egg noodles, divided

2½ cups (600 ml) vegetable oil

1 tsp salt

1 tbsp (14 g) butter

3 tbsp (45 ml) Wholesome Homemade Garlic Oil (page 125)

2½ tsp (10 g) grated fresh ginger

1½ tsp (3 g) cumin seeds

1½ tsp (3 g) ground cinnamon

1 tbsp (6 g) paprika

1 tbsp (5 g) ground coriander

1 tsp ground turmeric

1 green chili pepper, halved lengthwise

9 oz (252 g) boneless chicken breasts, cubed

3 tbsp (15 g) Thai red curry paste

2 cups (480 ml) Gut-Energizing Chicken Broth (page 122)

4 fresh lime leaves, or zest of 2 limes

¾ cup + 2 tsp (190 ml) coconut milk

3 tbsp (3 g) chopped fresh cilantro

If you're looking for the perfect Sunday meal to cook for the whole family, look no further. These Indian lamb shanks are especially delicious, and the meat literally falls off the bone. The lamb shanks cook for 2½ hours, allowing the flavors of the marinade to really infuse and give you that decadent and juicy meat.

Slow–Cooked Indian Lamb Shanks

YIELD: 3 TO 4 SERVINGS

Preheat your oven to 350°F (175°C). Set a rack in the middle-lower part of the oven.

Season the lamb shanks with the salt and pepper and make sure to really rub it into the meat. In a small bowl combine the coriander, garlic powder, paprika, turmeric and cumin seeds; stir well and set aside.

In a large oven-safe casserole dish (or a Dutch oven), melt the butter on medium heat. When it starts to sizzle, add in your lamb shanks. Sear the shanks for 3 to 4 minutes on each side, until they are a medium brown with some slightly darker parts. When your lamb shanks are a beautiful brown color, remove them from the pot and set them aside.

Add your onion to the same pot and simmer on low heat for 5 minutes. Then toss in the mixed spices as well as the cinnamon stick, cloves, bay leaves and red chili. When the spices become fragrant, after 5 to 8 minutes, add in the lamb shanks, balsamic vinegar, tomatoes and chicken broth. Cook on low heat for 15 minutes.

Remove the pot from the heat and put it in the oven for 2½ hours. Turn the lamb shanks every 30 minutes to make sure all sides are being cooked in the gravy.

When the lamb is done cooking, scoop out 1 cup (240 ml) of the sauce and place it in a small pot over medium heat. Add in the cornstarch and whisk quickly for 2 to 3 minutes. As soon as you see the gravy thicken, remove the pot from the heat. When you're ready to serve, drizzle the gravy over the lamb shanks and top with the chopped scallions.

20 oz (560 g) lamb shanks (2 large or 3 medium)

1 tsp coarse sea salt

2 tsp (4 g) black pepper

1½ tsp (4 g) ground coriander

1½ tsp (3 g) garlic powder

1 tsp paprika

1 tsp ground turmeric

1 tbsp (3 g) cumin seeds

1 tbsp + 1 tsp (19 g) butter

¾ cup (120 g) chopped onion

1 cinnamon stick

4 whole cloves

3 bay leaves

1 dried red chili pepper

2 tsp (10 ml) balsamic vinegar

4 oz (113 g) diced or crushed canned tomatoes

2 cups (480 ml) Gut-Energizing Chicken Broth (page 122)

1½ tsp (4 g) cornstarch

1 cup (100 g) chopped scallions

Tandoori chicken is a popular Indian and Pakistani dish, and one that is extremely flavorful. The sauce is made with yogurt as a base and mixed with many glorious spices. I always add in some orange food coloring because that's how you get that deep orange that we all think of with this dish. It's not necessary because the flavor is there either way, but it does look like the real deal when it comes out of the oven or off the barbecue.

Eastern–Influence Tandoori Chicken

YIELD: 2 TO 3 SERVINGS

Place the chicken in a medium bowl and add the vegetable oil, lemon juice, curry leaf, garlic, ginger, coriander, chili powder, salt, cayenne pepper, mayonnaise, yogurt and food coloring (if you choose to add it). Combine them together and stir so the chicken is completely coated. Cover the bowl with plastic wrap and refrigerate for 1 to 3 hours, or overnight for even better flavor.

Preheat your oven to 350°F (175°C). Line an oven rack with some tin foil and place it in the middle of the oven.

Put the chicken on the foil-lined rack. (If there is leftover marinade, do not throw it away; you will use it for basting.) Roast the chicken for 25 minutes, basting every so often with the marinade and flipping the chicken a few times so all sides get cooked evenly. I recommend flipping the chicken after about 15 minutes. Opening the oven will not affect the cooking process.

After 25 minutes, increase the heat to 400°F (200°C) and switch the oven to broil. Broil each side for 5 to 8 minutes, then remove the chicken from the oven and enjoy.

4 to 5 pieces bone-in chicken (breast, leg and thigh)

¼ cup (60 ml) vegetable oil

2 tsp (10 ml) lemon juice

1 curry leaf or 1 bay leaf

2 cloves garlic, crushed

1½-inch (4-cm) piece fresh ginger, minced

1 tbsp (6 g) ground coriander

1½ tsp (3 g) chili powder

¾ tsp salt

1½ tsp (3 g) cayenne pepper

1 tbsp (15 ml) mayonnaise

1 tbsp (15 ml) plain yogurt

1 tsp orange food coloring (optional)

The best part of this meal is how quickly it comes together. The flavor of the salmon is rich and comforting. It's an amazing food that is used often in low-FODMAP recipes because of its omega-3s and other fatty acids, as well as the fact that it doesn't cause any bloating or discomfort. This is a hearty meal that pairs with just about any vegetable and can be enjoyed by your whole family.

Pink Salmon Curry

YIELD: 2 TO 3 SERVINGS

In a medium pot over medium-high heat, add 3 cups (720 ml) of water, the potatoes and ½ teaspoon of salt. Bring the water to a boil and cook the potatoes for about 15 minutes, until they're soft (a fork should pierce the potatoes easily). Drain the water and set the potatoes aside.

Add the garlic oil and butter to another medium pot over medium heat. When the butter melts, add the shallots and sauté for 10 to 12 minutes until they are golden brown. Then add the boiled potatoes. Cook until the potatoes begin to brown, then add in the cumin seeds, peppercorns and green chili pepper and sauté for another 5 minutes.

Then add in the minced tomato, salmon (try not to break it up too much), ground cumin, turmeric, lemon juice and tomato paste. Cook for 15 to 20 minutes and then add in the broth and give it a good stir.

Meanwhile, in a separate pot, boil 2½ cups (600 ml) of water, then add ¾ teaspoon of salt and the rice. Stir to combine everything, cover the pot and then cook on medium-high heat for 15 to 20 minutes, until the rice is soft and most of the water has been absorbed. When the rice is cooked through, strain out any remaining water, return the rice to the pot and add a pat of butter on top of the rice. Reduce the heat to very low and cover with a lid for 7 minutes.

When the salmon is done, add the fresh cilantro and turn the heat off. Serve the curry on top of the rice and enjoy a warm and cozy meal.

4 oz (113 g) white potatoes, peeled and quartered

½ tsp + ¾ tsp (7 g) salt, divided

2 tsp (10 ml) Wholesome Homemade Garlic Oil (page 125)

1 tbsp (14 g) butter + more for the rice

¾ cup (120 g) chopped shallots

1½ tsp (3 g) cumin seeds

1½ tsp (3 g) whole black peppercorns

½ green chili pepper, seeded and chopped

½ cup (90 g) minced tomato

10½ oz (294 g) canned pink salmon, drained

1½ tsp (5 g) ground cumin

1 tsp ground turmeric

1 tsp freshly squeezed lemon juice

1½ tsp (8 g) tomato paste

⅓ cup + 1 tbsp (95 ml) Gut-Energizing Chicken Broth (page 122)

1½ cups (280 g) long-grain basmati rice

⅓ cup (5 g) chopped fresh cilantro

Soothing Sides and Staples

SIDE DISHES SHOULD NEVER GO *unnoticed. I find that even if I am making a very simple protein, I always need sweet potato fries on the side or something light to really complement my meal and give me the extra nourishment I need. This chapter is filled with all my absolute favorite side dishes; they can be paired with any main meal or even enjoyed as a snack on their own. I added two of the staples that I cannot live without—Wholesome Homemade Garlic Oil (page 125) and Gut-Energizing Chicken Broth (page 122)—which I use throughout this book. Both have amazing healing properties and benefits for IBS flare-ups and are also useful just to maintain a healthy lifestyle.*

The one thing I really love in a restaurant is when they serve fresh bread as soon as you've ordered. I am now bringing that right to your kitchen! The fresh herbs on top of the soft and fluffy dough really make this focaccia amazing. While it's still in the oven, you get that infectious warm bread smell. This herbed focaccia is vegan and can be dipped into soups, served as an appetizer or enjoyed just on its own.

Fresh Herbed Focaccia

YIELD: 4 TO 6 SERVINGS

In a small bowl, add the yeast and sugar, then pour in ¾ cup (180 ml) of warm water (about 68°F [20°C]). Give the mixture a good whisk and let it stand for 7 minutes. The yeast mixture will look murky with a few bubbles on top, but it won't foam much, so don't think that it hasn't been activated.

Grease a large bowl with some olive oil and set it aside.

In a stand mixer fitted with the dough hook or in a large bowl, add the flour, sea salt and garlic oil, then pour in the activated yeast mixture. Mix on low speed for 2 minutes to combine, or mix and stir with a wooden spoon until everything is well combined. When the ingredients have come together, turn the speed up to medium-high. It will take 5 to 7 minutes for the dough to pull away from the edges of the bowl and come together into a ball. If you're making this by hand, turn the dough out onto a lightly floured surface and knead until it comes together, about 10 minutes. When the dough forms a ball, place it in the greased bowl, cover with plastic wrap and leave it to rise for 1½ hours in a warm place.

When the dough is ready, add 2 teaspoons (10 ml) of olive oil to a medium ovenproof skillet or rectangular baking pan, and rub it all over the bottom and up the sides so the skillet is well greased. Place the dough in the skillet. Use your fingertips to stretch the dough out to the edges of the skillet. Drizzle the top with some more olive oil, cover the bowl with a tea towel and let the dough rise in a warm place for another 40 minutes.

Preheat your oven to 400°F (200°C).

When your focaccia has risen, evenly spread the olives, rosemary and thyme over the top. Use your fingertips to create dents in the focaccia so the olive oil can soak into the bread. Bake for 20 to 30 minutes, until the top is golden brown.

2 tsp (8 g) instant yeast

2 tsp (10 g) granulated sugar

2 tsp (10 ml) olive oil + more for greasing

2⅓ cups (290 g) all-purpose flour

¾ tsp coarse sea salt

2 tsp (10 ml) Wholesome Homemade Garlic Oil (page 125)

¼ cup (45 g) pitted olives, halved

3 tbsp (5 g) fresh rosemary leaves

3 tbsp (7 g) fresh thyme leaves

I have always loved coconut rice with curries, stews and just about anything— and this coconut sticky rice is going to make you fall in love with it too. The rice is cooked in coconut milk and sprinkled with desiccated coconut for a dish that is simply beautiful on the palate. The sugar really makes this side dish a treat, but the mango is the star of the show, bringing in color and a tart taste for a perfect contrast. This dish can be served as an appetizer, a side or enjoyed on its own (possibly even as dessert!).

Sticky Coconut Rice with Fresh Mangoes

YIELD: 3 TO 4 SERVINGS

Put the rice in a colander and rinse it three times with cold water. Set aside.

In a medium pot, bring the coconut milk and ⅔ cup (160 ml) of water to a boil over high heat. Add in the rice, lime leaves, 1 tablespoon (15 g) of sugar and the ¼ cup (20 g) desiccated coconut. Turn the heat down to low, cover the pot with a lid but leave it slightly ajar and simmer the rice for 10 to 12 minutes. When most of the liquid has been absorbed, turn the heat off, set the lid on tight and let the rice stand for 5 minutes.

In a small bowl, combine the cubed mango with the lemon juice and 1 teaspoon (5 g) of sugar. When you're ready to serve, stir the mango into the rice and top with the 2 tablespoons (11 g) desiccated coconut.

1 cup (190 g) short-grain basmati rice

1 cup + 2 tsp (250 ml) coconut milk

4 fresh or dried lime leaves or kaffir lime leaves, or zest of 2 limes

1 tbsp + 1 tsp (20 g) granulated sugar, divided

¼ cup + 2 tbsp (31 g) desiccated coconut, divided

½ cup (80 g) cubed fresh mango

2 tsp (10 ml) lemon juice

I find breadsticks to be so elegant! These cheesy twisted breadsticks are the perfect complement to your main meal, but they're also great for guests to snack on while they're awaiting dinner. I use two cheeses, as well as a touch of basil to make them absolutely delicious, and they can be prepared in just a few minutes with no fuss at all.

Sweet Basil Parmesan Breadsticks

YIELD: 3 TO 6 PEOPLE

Roll out your puff pastry on a floured surface, being careful not to roll it too thin. It should be at least 1 inch (2.5 cm) thick—no thinner. Arrange the pastry so the long sides are horizontal and parallel to your body.

Preheat your oven to 350°F (175°C). Line a baking sheet with parchment paper and lightly spray it with nonstick cooking spray.

Whisk the eggs in a small bowl. Using a pastry brush, brush the pastry all over with the egg wash, leaving a ½-inch (1.3-cm) border all around. (You should have some egg wash left over; set it aside.) Sprinkle both cheeses over the pastry, followed by the garlic powder and basil. With both hands, lightly press the toppings down into the pastry so that they are less likely to move when you cut and twist the dough.

Using a pizza cutter or a sharp knife, cut the dough from top to bottom into 2-inch (5-cm)-wide strips. Working with one strip at a time, twist the strip clockwise with one hand and counter-clockwise with the other, creating a twisted tube. You don't need to twist it too much, just enough so that it will hold its shape. Pinch the ends to solidify the shape and place it on the baking sheet. Continue until you have shaped all the breadsticks. Lightly brush them with the remainder of the egg wash.

Bake for 15 to 25 minutes. When the pastry has become golden brown and the cheese begins to turn dark orange, remove the pan from the oven. Let the breadsticks cool for 10 minutes, then enjoy.

10½ oz (294 g) frozen puff pastry, defrosted

All-purpose flour, for rolling

Nonstick cooking spray

2 eggs

½ cup (50 g) grated Parmesan cheese

⅓ cup (30 g) grated Manchego cheese

2 tsp (5 g) garlic powder

1½ tbsp (7 g) dried basil

Sweet potato wedges are my not-so-guilty pleasure because they are packed with amazing health benefits, one being that they promote gut health due to their fiber and antioxidants. So while you are snacking away on these salted, thyme-infused wedges, you are also benefiting your body by giving it relief and satisfaction at the same time. These wedges are an amazing accompaniment to a burger, but I must admit, I love eating them all on their own.

Salted Thyme Sweet Potato Wedges

YIELD: 2 TO 3 SERVINGS

Preheat your oven to 400°F (200°C). Line a baking sheet with foil, shiny side facing down.

Drizzle half the oil onto the foil and then place the sweet potato wedges on top. Add the salt, garlic powder, parsley, paprika and thyme and toss everything together with a spatula or with your hands. Drizzle the rest of the oil over the sweet potatoes to make sure they get extra crispy.

Bake for 30 to 40 minutes, tossing every 10 minutes so the sweet potatoes can brown evenly. Remove the pan from the oven, being careful, as it will be hot. The sweet potatoes should be slightly charred on some parts and crisp on the corners—that's when you know they're done. Sprinkle them with more flaky sea salt, if desired.

4 tbsp (60 ml) olive oil, divided

2 medium sweet potatoes, peeled and cut into 2-inch (5-cm) wedges

1 tsp flaky sea salt + more to sprinkle

2 tsp (5 g) garlic powder

2 tbsp (8 g) chopped fresh Italian parsley

2½ tsp (5 g) paprika

1 tbsp + 1 tsp (4 g) dried thyme

This creamy mushroom ragù goes with everything. I love it with either a sweet potato mash or with Salted Thyme Sweet Potato Wedges (page 110)—but once you taste it, you'll see how versatile it is. The fresh thyme really lifts this dish, and smelling those fresh herbs adds a very natural and organic element, which I love in all dishes. For my barbecue seasoning mix, I like the one from K.C. Rib Doctor.

Thyme–Infused Mushroom Ragù

YIELD: 2 TO 3 SERVINGS

Wipe the mushrooms with a dry paper towel to clean off the dirt, then cut them into quarters. In a medium bowl, toss the mushrooms with the barbecue seasoning.

Warm a medium pan over medium heat and add the oil. Add the mushrooms to the warmed pan and cook, stirring occasionally. When they start to brown, after about 7 minutes, add in the thyme, coconut cream and crème fraîche. Turn the heat to low and simmer until the cream gets thick, 8 to 10 minutes. Add the salt and pepper, then serve hot.

8 oz (224 g) fresh porcini mushrooms

3 tbsp (21 g) barbecue seasoning mix

1 tbsp (15 ml) olive oil

4 sprigs fresh thyme

½ cup (120 ml) coconut cream

1 tbsp (15 ml) crème fraîche

⅓ tsp salt

1½ tsp (3 g) pepper

If you're one of those people who really enjoy a good salad (much like me), either as a side dish or a main, then you are going to absolutely love this recipe. The amount of kale seems small, but it adds a delicate crunch with every bite, as well as the benefit of being high in vitamin C and helping to lower cholesterol levels. The highlight of this salad, however, has to be the vinaigrette. It has subtle hints of honey, apple cider vinegar and Dijon mustard, which give it a sweet but tangy flavor that truly complements the salad.

Any Season Chicken Kale Salad

YIELD: 3 TO 4 SERVINGS

To make the vinaigrette, add all the ingredients to a medium jar with a tight-fitting lid. Close the lid and give the jar a good shake, or stir the ingredients with a spoon.

To make the salad, in a medium bowl, combine the paprika, salt, red pepper, Cajun spice, thyme and basil and toss with the chicken. Rub the spices into the chicken.

In a medium pan, add the garlic oil over medium heat. Add the chicken and spices and cook for about 10 minutes, stirring. Toss in the mushrooms and cook for 5 to 8 minutes more. When the chicken is a golden brown color, remove the pan from the heat.

In a colander, rinse the kale, arugula and tomatoes and place them on a serving platter. Place the chicken and mushrooms on top of the greens, followed by the feta cheese. Drizzle the dressing on top and toss everything together to combine. Then sprinkle the pine nuts on top for some crunch.

VINAIGRETTE

4 tsp (20 ml) Wholesome Homemade Garlic Oil (page 125)

1 tsp apple cider vinegar

1 tbsp + 1 tsp (20 ml) honey

¾ tsp balsamic vinegar

1 tsp Dijon mustard

CHICKEN SALAD

1½ tsp (3 g) paprika

½ tsp coarse sea salt

1 tsp crushed red pepper

1½ tsp (3 g) Cajun spice blend

1½ tsp (2 g) dried thyme

1½ tsp (2 g) dried basil

10 oz (280 g) boneless, skinless chicken breasts, cut into strips

1 tbsp (15 ml) Wholesome Homemade Garlic Oil (page 125)

²/₃ cup (50 g) chopped mushrooms

1 cup (60 g) chopped kale

½ cup (10 g) arugula

½ cup (75 g) chopped tomatoes

¼ cup (30 g) crumbled feta cheese

2½ tbsp (20 g) toasted pine nuts

These zucchini fritters are such a glorious and savory treat. They have a great salty tang, as well as a hint of the Mediterranean from the basil pesto. (You can store any leftover pesto in an airtight container in the fridge for up to two weeks. Use it as a sauce with any pasta you like for a very quick meal.) I love adding zucchini to almost anything I eat because its soft fiber promotes a healthy gut— therefore, no IBS flare-ups. Incorporating gut-healthy vegetables in every meal can really build a strong gut over time, so zucchini is definitely one to keep in your kitchen.

Indulgent Zucchini Fritters with Basil Pesto

YIELD: 3 TO 4 SERVINGS

Make the pesto first. In a food processor with the blade attachment, combine the chives, basil, garlic oil, pine nuts, Parmesan cheese, lemon juice and salt and blitz for 3 to 5 minutes until smooth. There will still be small bits of chopped leaves, and this is fine.

To make the fritters, rinse and grate the zucchini into a large bowl, add the ½ teaspoon of salt and give it a good but gentle mix. Then place the zucchini in a colander set over the bowl to allow it to drain and absorb the salt for 10 minutes. Put the grated zucchini in a tea towel or muslin cloth. Bring the corners of the cloth together, hold it over the sink and twist. Tighten the cloth to strain out as much liquid as you can. Place the strained zucchini in a medium bowl and set aside.

To the bowl of zucchini, add the basil pesto, Parmesan cheese, spinach, flour, egg, paprika, ½ teaspoon of salt, basil, thyme, pepper and 1 tablespoon (15 ml) olive oil. Using a wooden spoon, stir to combine.

In a medium skillet, add 1 tablespoon (15 ml) of olive oil over medium heat. Using a tablespoon, scoop out the zucchini batter and place it into the warmed pan. You may have to work in batches. Each fritter should be circular, so use a spatula or the back of the spoon if you need to spread it out. Fry for 3 to 5 minutes on each side. When the color is golden to medium brown, remove the fritters from the pan and place them on a paper towel to drain the excess oil. Repeat until you have used up all the zucchini batter. Add more oil to the pan if needed. Serve the fritters warm and enjoy!

BASIL PESTO

¾ cup (40 g) chopped chives

1 cup (25 g) fresh basil

½ cup (120 ml) Wholesome Homemade Garlic Oil (page 125)

½ cup (35 g) pine nuts

¼ cup (25 g) grated Parmesan cheese

1 tsp lemon juice

½ tsp salt

ZUCCHINI FRITTERS

12 oz (340 g) zucchini

1 tsp salt, divided

2 tbsp (30 ml) basil pesto (see above)

½ cup (50 g) grated Parmesan cheese

1 cup (30 g) chopped baby spinach

1 cup (125 g) all-purpose flour

1 egg

1½ tsp (3 g) paprika

2 tsp (3 g) dried basil

1 tbsp (3 g) dried thyme

1½ tsp (3 g) pepper

2 tbsp (30 ml) olive oil, divided

Acorn squash is another soft fiber that promotes gut health, so I love incorporating it into my meals. I fill the squash halves with a caramelized vegetable chutney, brown rice and grated zucchini. I love that I get my vegetables in for the day while taking care of my body. As a bonus, you can keep the leftover chutney in the fridge for three to four weeks. I love it as a side to any curry, and I suggest pairing it with the Pink Salmon Curry (page 100) as well.

Stuffed Acorn Squash with Brown Rice and Chutney

YIELD: 4 SERVINGS

To make the chutney, first wash and set aside several heatproof glass jars with tight-fitting lids. You'll need enough jars for about 3¼ cups (780 ml) in total.

In a large saucepan, combine the tomatoes, spring onion, zucchini, brown sugar, vinegar, salt, garlic oil, turmeric and coriander and bring to a simmer on medium heat, stirring frequently. After 15 to 20 minutes, when the juices from the tomato start to evaporate and the liquid begins to reduce, turn the heat to low. Continue cooking for about 1 hour, stirring frequently. When the chutney is ready, remove it from the heat, spoon it immediately into glass jars, close the lids and set the jars aside to cool.

To make the squash, preheat your oven to 350°F (175°C). Line a baking sheet with parchment paper.

Add your rice, zucchini, garlic oil, Cajun spice, thyme and chutney to a medium bowl and mix well. Spoon the filling into the squash halves, filling them all evenly. Drizzle the olive oil over the top of the filling. Put the stuffed squash on the baking sheet.

Roast the squash for 30 to 40 minutes. Test the softness with a fork to make sure it's soft and cooked through. The squash will be hot, so allow it to cool for 10 minutes before eating.

CHUTNEY

1½ lbs (680 g) ripe medium tomatoes, cut in half

1 cup (50 g) finely chopped spring onion, green parts only

1½ cups (200 g) finely diced zucchini

⅓ cup + 2 tbsp (100 g) brown sugar

¼ cup (60 ml) apple cider vinegar

½ tsp salt

2 tbsp (30 ml) Wholesome Homemade Garlic Oil (page 125)

1 tsp ground turmeric

1½ tsp (3 g) ground coriander

ACORN SQUASH

½ cup (100 g) cooked brown rice

½ cup (60 g) finely chopped zucchini

2 tbsp (30 ml) Wholesome Homemade Garlic Oil (page 125)

2½ tsp (5 g) Cajun spice blend

1 tbsp (3 g) dried thyme

4 tbsp (60 ml) chutney (see above)

2 large acorn squash, cut in half and seeded

¼ cup (60 ml) olive oil

Chicken strips are easy to make, and once the oil is hot, it's just the best thing to drop in your chicken and see it sizzle away. The dipping sauce is light, packed with flavor and is made with ingredients you probably already have on hand. If you have some sauce left over, save it for later to spread on sandwiches or use as a salad dressing.

Panko–Crusted Chicken Strips with Garlic Sriracha Sauce

YIELD: 2 TO 4 SERVINGS

Place the flour in a small, shallow bowl. Whisk your eggs in a separate small bowl. Add the bread crumbs to one more small, shallow bowl. In the bowl with the bread crumbs, add in the garlic powder, paprika, cayenne pepper, thyme, cumin, Parmesan cheese, salt and barbecue seasoning, and stir to combine.

Heat the oil to 375°F (190°C) in a small pot. When you have reached the correct temperature, working with one chicken strip at a time, dip the chicken into the flour first, dusting off any excess. Then dip it into the egg and finally into the bread crumb mixture so it's fully coated. Fry the strips two at a time so you don't overcrowd the pot, 2 to 3 minutes on each side. When the bread crumbs turn a medium golden brown, you know they are fully cooked through. Put them on a plate lined with paper towels to absorb any excess oil.

Cover the fried chicken strips with a foil tent to keep them warm while you quickly make your dipping sauce. In a small pot, melt the butter. In a small bowl, mix the mayonnaise, sriracha, garlic oil, thyme, pepper and mustard. Stir in the melted butter. When everything has been mixed together well, you can proceed to dipping and eating your chicken strips.

CHICKEN STRIPS

1 cup (125 g) all-purpose flour

2 eggs

1¾ cups (100 g) panko bread crumbs

1 tbsp (8 g) garlic powder

1 tbsp (8 g) paprika

1½ tsp (4 g) cayenne pepper

3 tbsp (8 g) dried thyme

1 tbsp (5 g) ground cumin

⅓ cup (33 g) grated Parmesan cheese

½ tsp salt

1 tbsp + 1 tsp (8 g) barbecue seasoning mix

3 cups (720 ml) vegetable oil

3 boneless, skinless chicken breasts, cut into 1½-inch (4-cm)-thick strips

GARLIC SRIRACHA SAUCE

2 tsp (9 g) butter

⅓ cup (80 ml) mayonnaise

2 tbsp (30 ml) sriracha

2 tsp (10 ml) Wholesome Homemade Garlic Oil (page 125)

1 tbsp (3 g) dried thyme

1½ tsp (3 g) black pepper

½ tsp Dijon mustard

A good homemade chicken broth recipe is probably one of the best things you can have for your health. Not only is it more cost-effective to make and store it yourself, but the broth helps to alleviate joint pain, improves bone growth and above all, is a major powerhouse as an anti-inflammatory. Drinking homemade broth could actually ease the effects of IBS once you start feeling that discomfort. I use this recipe often in this cookbook because it has so much flavor and really elevates every recipe here. Freezing is a good option, so you can make a big batch and use it as you need it.

Gut-Energizing Chicken Broth

YIELD: 2½ QUARTS (2.3 L)

Lay your chicken on its back on a cutting board and cut in a straight line through the center, starting from the neck and cutting down through the breast bone. Pull the two sides of the breast apart and open the chicken up. Remove all the giblets and soft matter and thoroughly rinse the insides of the chicken. Put it in a large stock pot.

Add the celery, onion, carrots, leeks, bok choy, bay leaves, peppercorns and salt. Then add 3 quarts (3 L) of water and stir to mix everything.

Put the pot on the largest burner on your stove, cover it with a lid, and set the heat to medium-low. Cook for 1 hour, making sure to stir every so often. Then lower the heat to low and cook for another 20 minutes. When the broth has turned a light brown/green and the chicken easily falls off the bone, you know your broth is ready.

Strain the broth so that all the solid pieces are removed and allow it to come to room temperature. When your broth is cooled, you can either put it in containers and freeze half of it or you can put it in tightly sealed jars in the fridge. It will keep in the refrigerator for 4 to 5 days and in the freezer for 1 month.

1 whole raw chicken

2 stalks celery, trimmed and halved across

1 whole onion, with the skin, cut into quarters

½ cup (64 g) chopped carrots

1½ oz (42 g) leeks, trimmed and halved across

3 heads baby bok choy

3 bay leaves

2 tsp (4 g) whole peppercorns

1 tbsp (18 g) salt

This recipe is a staple for me, and it's one I have relied on almost every day since adapting my lifestyle to account for IBS. You will notice that instead of garlic in many of the recipes in this book, you will find garlic oil. That's because garlic in its whole form (cooked or uncooked) can trigger an IBS flare-up. But garlic oil provides the same flavor without any side effects; the more oil you add, the more intense the flavor. I don't even miss using garlic anymore.

Wholesome Homemade Garlic Oil

YIELD: 1½ CUPS (360 ML)

Peel the garlic cloves so all the skins are removed: Using a wide knife, press down on each clove with some pressure until the garlic clove pops and spreads out, exposing the inside. Do this with all the cloves.

In a small pot over medium heat, add the garlic and olive oil. When the garlic starts to fry, reduce the heat to low. Cook for 10 to 12 minutes, stirring every few minutes. When the garlic starts to turn medium to dark brown, remove the pot from the heat and leave the garlic to sit in the oil for 1 hour. Strain out all the solids and leave the oil to cool.

When it is cool, store the oil in an airtight container in a dry place for up to 1 month.

1 head garlic

1½ cups (360 ml) extra-virgin olive oil

The Dessert Station

AS A CHEF, *I have a soft spot for all things sweet and decadent. But for this chapter, I've migrated away from incorporating a lot of sugar while still giving you enough to satisfy your sweet tooth. These recipes are made with such wholesome ingredients, and the sugar in each dessert is just the right amount for you to enjoy without triggering flare-ups. I truly believe desserts should be enjoyed, and this chapter is one to celebrate and allow yourself to appreciate each sweet treat you make.*

Dark chocolate brings a healthy decadence to your palate, and when you take a bite of these brownies, you will find a delightfully moist cake studded with pops of hazelnuts. This recipe has just enough sugar to make it sweet, but not enough to be unhealthy or trigger inflammation. This will be a favorite in your home, not just for yourself but for everyone who tries it.

Decadent Dark Chocolate Crinkle Brownies
YIELD: 12 TO 16 BROWNIES

Preheat your oven to 350°F (175°C). Line an 8 x 8–inch (20 x 20–cm) baking pan with parchment paper and spray with nonstick cooking spray.

In a small pot, melt the butter on medium heat. When it begins to foam, stir it a few times to diffuse the foam and allow the butter to brown. This should take 5 to 8 minutes. When the butter starts to brown, wait about 20 seconds and then take it off the heat. It will continue to brown a bit.

In a small bowl, add the dark chocolate along with the vanilla extract, almond extract and cocoa powder. Add the mixture to the pot with the butter and stir with a wooden spoon until combined.

In a stand mixer with the whisk attachment, or using a handheld electric mixer and a large bowl, whisk together the confectioner's sugar, brown sugar and eggs for 5 to 10 minutes on medium to high speed. When the mixture becomes thick and pale yellow, turn the mixer to low speed and slowly pour in the chocolate mixture in a steady stream. Mix on low speed until just combined.

Using a spatula, fold in the flour and chopped hazelnuts very gently. Mix until there are no more flour streaks. Pour the batter into the prepared pan and spread it out evenly with the spatula.

Bake for 35 to 40 minutes, then let the brownies cool in the pan for 15 to 20 minutes before cutting.

Nonstick cooking spray

⅓ cup + 1 tsp (80 g) butter

1 cup (170 g) chopped dark chocolate (70% cocoa or more)

1 tsp vanilla extract

1 tsp almond extract

3 tbsp (14 g) unsweetened cocoa powder

¾ cup (90 g) confectioner's sugar

½ cup (100 g) brown sugar

3 eggs

1 cup (125 g) all-purpose flour

½ cup (50 g) chopped hazelnuts

When it comes to teatime, I am here for the treats, the tea and the company. These muffins are more like cupcakes, with their gorgeous soft and moist texture. They are the perfect dessert, but I enjoy them with my morning coffee as well. Best of all, the streusel on top is so easy to make.

Tea-Time Coffee Streusel Muffins

YIELD: 12 MUFFINS

Preheat the oven to 350°F (175°C). Line a 12-cup muffin tin with cupcake liners and spray them with nonstick cooking spray. Set aside.

In a medium bowl, whisk together the salt, baking soda, baking powder, cinnamon and flour and set aside. In a small bowl, combine the milk and yogurt and set aside.

In a stand mixer with a paddle attachment, or using a handheld electric mixer and a large bowl, beat together the butter, granulated sugar and brown sugar until the mixture is very thick and light in color, 6 to 9 minutes on high speed. Add your vanilla and eggs to the butter mixture. Then add half the flour mixture into the batter and beat for a few moments. Follow that with half the yogurt mixture. Repeat until all the flour and yogurt mixtures have been added.

In a small bowl, combine the coffee granules with 1 tablespoon (15 ml) of warm water and add it to the batter. Whisk one last time for a few seconds just to combine everything.

Using a spatula, gently fold in half the chocolate chips until just combined. Make sure not to overmix. When there are no more streaks of flour or coffee, scoop the batter into the cupcake liners until they are three-quarters full. Top with the remaining chocolate chips.

To make the streusel, in a medium bowl combine the flour, cinnamon and brown sugar and whisk. Add in the cubed butter, and mix with your fingertips until it becomes crumbly and light in color. Squeeze the streusel between your hands to create varying size chunks, and then release with your fingertips. Sprinkle on top of the muffins before baking.

Bake the muffins for 18 to 20 minutes. When a toothpick inserted in the center comes out clean and the tops are golden brown, remove from the oven and enjoy.

MUFFINS

Nonstick cooking spray

½ tsp salt

½ tsp baking soda

1 tsp baking powder

1½ tsp (3 g) ground cinnamon

½ cup (60 g) all-purpose flour

1 tbsp (15 ml) whole milk

⅔ cup + 2 tsp (170 ml) plain yogurt

2 tbsp (28 g) butter, softened

3 tbsp (40 g) granulated sugar

2 tbsp (30 g) brown sugar

2 tsp (10 ml) vanilla extract

2 eggs

1 tsp instant coffee granules

2 tbsp (20 g) chocolate chips, divided

STREUSEL

⅓ cup (40 g) all-purpose flour

1 tsp ground cinnamon

½ cup (100 g) brown sugar

¼ cup (56 g) cold butter, cubed

I love blondies—the golden version of brownies. These are made with a peanut butter base and topped with chocolate chips to really give you a sweet moment during the day. This is a very easy recipe and one that I love! The oat flour is perfect for a low-FODMAP lifestyle and the added cinnamon has anti-inflammatory properties for a healthy gut.

Healthy Glowing Blondies

YIELD: 9 BLONDIES

Preheat the oven to 350°F (175°C). Line an 8 x 8–inch (20 x 20–cm) baking pan with parchment paper and spray with a nonstick cooking spray.

In a large bowl, whisk together the peanut butter, coconut sugar, molasses, milk and vanilla. Using a spatula or a wooden spoon, stir in the oat flour, salt, cinnamon and baking powder until the batter becomes thick. Pour the batter into the baking pan, top with chocolate chunks and bake for 20 to 25 minutes. When the edges begin to brown you can remove the pan from the oven.

Cool in the pan for 25 minutes before removing the blondies. Sprinkle on the flaky sea salt for a sweet and salty accent. Cut into squares and enjoy your dessert whenever you want.

Nonstick cooking spray

½ cup + 2 tbsp (160 g) peanut butter

⅓ cup + 2 tbsp (95 g) coconut sugar

1 tbsp (15 ml) molasses

⅓ cup (80 ml) whole milk

1 tsp vanilla extract

1 cup (85 g) fine oat flour

½ tsp salt

1½ tsp (3 g) ground cinnamon

½ tsp baking powder

3 tbsp (35 g) chocolate chunks

¾ tsp flaky sea salt

Making a delicious cake in a mug in the microwave has to be the best idea ever! This cake takes less than 10 minutes to make, and it is perfect for those days when you need a quick sweet fix. When I came up with this recipe, I felt that it needed to be simple, tasty and above all, moist. No one likes a dense cake, even if it's in a mug. This is made with unsweetened cocoa, which adds a much-needed bitterness to the peanut butter and chocolate chips. Top with more peanut butter or ice cream, if you like.

Peanut Butter Chocolate Chip Mug Cake

YIELD: 1 SERVING

In a small bowl, whisk together the flour, cocoa powder, baking powder, cinnamon and 3 tablespoons (30 g) of chocolate chips. In a separate small bowl, whisk together the milk and vegetable oil, then pour them into the dry ingredients and whisk until there are no lumps.

Pour half the batter into a standard size coffee mug, then add your peanut butter. Fill the mug up with the remaining batter. Top with 2 teaspoons (5 g) of chocolate chips.

Microwave on high for 30 seconds to 1 minute. When the cake begins to rise, wait a few seconds and then remove it from the microwave. Melt the remaining dark chocolate in the microwave and drizzle it over the cake for even more decadence.

¼ cup (31 g) all-purpose flour

1 tbsp (5 g) unsweetened cocoa powder

1 tsp baking powder

1½ tsp (3 g) ground cinnamon

3 tbsp + 2 tsp (35 g) dark chocolate chips, for topping

¼ cup + 1 tbsp (75 ml) whole milk

2 tbsp (30 ml) vegetable oil

1 tbsp (16 g) crunchy or smooth peanut butter

These sweet Jam Tarts are inspired by the classic Pop-Tart. They have a light, biscuit-like pastry and the filling is a super easy homemade strawberry jam. This recipe has very little sugar, so it won't irritate your gut. Removing sugar completely from your diet can be tough, so I'd rather reduce the amount to a tolerable level while still making a delicious and enjoyable treat! This recipe makes more jam than you can use up in the tarts. Put the rest in a jar and store in the fridge for up to 1 month.

Strawberry Jam Tarts

YIELD: 5 TO 6 TARTS

Start by making the pastry. In a food processor, add in the flour, sugar and salt. Blitz for a few seconds just to combine. Divide the butter into 4 equal portions and add it to the food processor, a portion at a time, blitzing in between each addition and allowing it to break down. When all the butter has been added, the mixture should be very smooth and a pale-yellow color.

Pour in half the ice water and blitz for 15 seconds. The pastry should look like it's coming together. Then slowly add in the rest of the water. Be careful to not throw it all in at once, as you may only need a few tablespoons more. The final result should be a soft, buttery pastry that comes together easily and there should be very few flour bits visible.

Turn the dough out onto a floured surface, knead for about 1 minute, then flatten and form it into a round disk. Cover it with plastic wrap and let it chill in the fridge for 30 minutes.

While the pastry chills, make the jam. Place the strawberries in a medium pot along with the lemon juice and sugar. Stir and then turn the heat to medium-low. Simmer for 30 to 40 minutes. Stir every so often to make sure nothing is sticking to the bottom of the pot. If there is some sticking, add 1 tablespoon (15 ml) of water and stir. The strawberries should break down and the sauce should be thick. Spoon out the jam into a heatproof bowl or jar and allow it to cool at room temperature.

Preheat your oven to 350°F (175°C). Line two baking sheets with parchment paper.

(Continued)

PASTRY

2½ cups (310 g) all-purpose flour + more for rolling

2 tsp (10 g) granulated sugar

½ tsp salt

¾ cup + 1 tbsp (182 g) salted butter, cold and cubed

⅓ cup + 2 tsp (95 ml) ice water

2 eggs

JAM

2⅓ cups (350 g) fresh strawberries, trimmed and halved

2 tbsp + 1 tsp (35 ml) lemon juice

¾ cup (150 g) granulated sugar

When the pastry is chilled, roll it into a rectangle (roughly 9 x 12 inches [23 x 30 cm]) and then cut the large rectangle into 10 to 12 smaller rectangles. They will pair up, so make sure they are similar in size. On every other rectangle, spread 1 to 2 tablespoons (20 to 40 g) of cooled jam, leaving some room around the edges that is jam free. Place another rectangle on top, seal and flatten the edges down with a fork. Place the tarts on the baking sheets with about 1 inch (2.5 cm) between them.

Whisk the eggs in a small bowl to create an egg wash and brush the top of each tart. Place the baking sheets with the tarts in the fridge for 30 minutes. Then place the sheets in the oven and bake the tarts for 25 minutes. When they're ready, they should be a golden brown color on top and the pastry should be light brown on the bottom.

Allow them to cool down for 20 minutes. In the meantime, make the topping. In a small bowl, whisk together the confectioner's sugar, lemon juice and jam. Drizzle onto the cooled tarts and enjoy.

1 cup (120 g) confectioner's sugar

2 tsp (10 ml) lemon juice

1 to 2 tbsp (20 to 40 g) strawberry jam

Apple cider vinegar has so many health benefits, and I love it because the process used to make it reduces the levels of fructose and sorbitol found in the apples, thereby making it amazing for a low-FODMAP diet. The apple cider vinegar flavor is ever so slight in this recipe, and the sugar coating balances it very nicely. I love that these donuts are baked, making them so much healthier for you to enjoy.

Baked Apple Cider Donuts

YIELD: 8 TO 12 DONUTS

Preheat your oven to 350°F (175°C). Spray a 12-hole donut pan with nonstick cooking spray.

In a small pot, bring the apple cider vinegar, cinnamon stick, cardamom pods and star anise to a boil on medium-high heat. When the apple cider vinegar has boiled down to about ½ cup (120 ml), after 20 to 25 minutes, remove from the heat and discard the cinnamon stick, cardamom pods and star anise pods. Set the liquid aside.

In a medium bowl combine your flour, baking soda, baking powder, ground cinnamon, nutmeg, salt and ground cardamom and give it a good whisk to combine everything.

Then in a separate medium bowl, whisk together the egg, melted butter, brown sugar, granulated sugar and milk. Add this to the dry ingredients using a spatula or wooden spoon and fold to incorporate. Then add in the apple cider reduction.

When everything is combined (do not overmix), pipe the batter into the donut pan using a piping bag, or pour the batter in a plastic food storage bag, snip off a bottom corner and pipe it that way. Bake for 11 to 13 minutes. When the tops are nicely browned, you can remove the pan from the oven. Cool in the pan for 10 minutes, then place the donuts on a wire rack to cool completely.

When the donuts have cooled for 15 minutes, make the topping. Combine the sugar and cinnamon in a medium bowl. Put the melted coconut oil in a separate shallow bowl. Dip the top of each donut into the coconut oil and then into the sugar mixture.

DONUTS

Nonstick cooking spray

1 cup (240 ml) apple cider vinegar

1 cinnamon stick

2 cardamom pods

2 star anise pods

2 cups (250 g) all-purpose flour

½ tsp baking soda

½ tsp baking powder

1½ tsp (4 g) ground cinnamon

1½ tsp (3 g) ground nutmeg

⅓ tsp salt

1½ tsp (3 g) ground cardamom

1 egg

2 tbsp + 1 tsp (33 g) melted butter

½ cup (110 g) brown sugar

⅓ cup (66 g) granulated sugar

¾ cup (180 ml) whole milk

TOPPING

⅓ cup (66 g) granulated sugar

1 tbsp (10 g) ground cinnamon

½ cup (120 ml) melted coconut oil

This banana date loaf is so light and tastes of fresh, sweet dates and cinnamon, both of which are calming for our bodies. This is such a simple recipe, and after you've made it once, it's really hard to stop because it will immediately become a fan favorite in your home. The banana flavor is subtle but makes the loaf moist and soft, and the lemony glaze balances all the other flavors.

Decadent Banana and Date Loaf

YIELD: 8 TO 10 SLICES

Preheat your oven to 350°F (175°C). Place a rack in the middle of the oven. Line a standard 8 x 4–inch (20 x 10–cm) loaf pan with parchment paper and then spray it with nonstick cooking spray.

Put the dates in a medium bowl and pour 1¼ cups (300 ml) of boiling water over them. Soak the dates for 10 minutes. When they are soft, drain, roughly chop them and set them aside.

In a medium bowl, whisk together the flour, baking soda, baking powder, salt, cinnamon and nutmeg and set aside.

Pour the melted butter into a large bowl. Add the brown sugar and granulated sugar and whisk for about 1 minute. Add the bananas to the butter mixture and give it a good whisk, then add in the eggs, yogurt and vanilla and whisk to combine. Using a spatula, add half the flour mixture to the wet ingredients. Stir to combine and then add in the rest. Then fold in the dates.

Scoop the batter into the prepared loaf pan and bake for 55 to 65 minutes. Check after 45 minutes and if the top starts to burn, place a sheet of parchment paper over the top. When a toothpick inserted in the center comes out clean, your loaf is ready. Turn it out onto a wire rack and cool.

While the loaf cools, make the glaze. In a small bowl, whisk together the confectioner's sugar and lemon juice until you have a thick and creamy glaze. When the loaf has cooled completely, lightly drizzle the glaze over the top.

LOAF

Nonstick cooking spray

3 oz (84 g) Medjool dates, pitted

2¼ cups (280 g) all-purpose flour

½ tsp baking soda

¾ tsp baking powder

½ tsp salt

1 tsp ground cinnamon

1 tsp ground nutmeg

½ cup (120 ml) butter, melted

⅔ cup (140 g) brown sugar

2 tbsp + 2 tsp (40 g) granulated sugar

3 overripe medium bananas, mashed

2 eggs

½ cup (120 ml) plain yogurt

1 tsp vanilla extract

GLAZE

¾ cup (90 g) confectioner's sugar

2 tbsp (30 ml) lemon juice

Acknowledgments

Before anything else, I have to thank the Almighty for blessing me with this opportunity to create and above all to share what I've learned with you all. I always saw suffering from IBS as a negative, but when this opportunity arose, I knew God gave me this to share with the world the ways in which I live with it and overcome it every day. It is a true blessing to be able to share recipes that can aid in your health and lifestyle, and in some small way make it that much easier to wake up every day knowing that you don't need to feel that discomfort or pain any longer. *Alhamdulliah* (Praise be to God).

Thank you to my dear mother, who to this day believes in me. She sent me to Le Cordon Bleu and supported my decision to leave law school, although it wasn't an easy decision (she is a lawyer, so naturally she wanted me to follow in her big footsteps). She helped me move to London at age twenty-three, which was my first time leaving home, and never stopped being my biggest cheerleader. I love you with all my heart, and my gratitude to you can never fully be put into words.

My whole family really pushed me to where I am today, and I thank them (my mom, dad and sister, Lailaa) for never criticizing my choice in career even when it was sometimes hard for them to understand. They were my pillar in my earlier years when I was still finding my place in the world, and they made it easy to come home from London and really trust that I knew what I was doing, even when some days felt harder than others.

My darling husband, Junaid, I could write an essay about what you have done for me in my life. You saw me through dark times and still never left my side. You shot every recipe in this book, while putting projects aside to prioritize my dream. You cooked and took care of me when all I wanted to do was give up. You stayed up late at night with me, making sure I completed the chapters I set out for that day. You were my greatest taste tester, and when things were not up to standard, you were never afraid of letting me know, if only to better myself and these recipes. Might I add that this was our first year of marriage and living together during a pandemic. You make being a good husband look easy, and I thank God every day for sending you to me. I love you, bubi.

Aunty Zuraida, Uncle Ismail and Aunty Hamida, you will never truly know how much you inspired me. I have the privilege of being gifted your mother's name (my maternal grandmother), who to this day is well known for her amazing baking and cooking skills. I keep you in my heart every day while I pursue my dream. You were there and whispered words of affirmation to me, unbeknownst to many but much acknowledged by me, your niece. *Shukran* (thank you).

To my best friend, Zubi, you've done more for me than you know. We traveled the world together, got lost in our career direction for a moment and while most of our friendship was long-distance, it always felt like you were right next to me giving me a hug. I can't express how grateful I am to you for your kindness and generosity. You are one hell of a best friend, to the point where you brought me coffee at 6 a.m. on my wedding day, and did the same for the submission deadline for my manuscript. Thank you for everything.

To my publisher, Page Street Publishing, you may not know this but when I received that email from Caitlin, I was at a crossroads with my career and didn't feel like I was making much of an impact. This opportunity gave me the push I needed to be the best version of myself, and I thank you deeply for gifting me with this, as well as believing in me.

This book is dedicated to you, everyone who makes a recipe, purchases my cookbook, likes a photograph, tells a friend about this book and who feels some comfort knowing they aren't alone. Thank you for being here in this space and taking the time in your busy lives to read this cookbook. I want you to know that I made it for us, so we can feel liberated from the stereotype that others may have placed upon us. We are beautiful, our bodies are incredible and we take each day as it comes, as warriors.

So thank you a thousand times over.

About the Author

Zorah Booley is a food blogger and chef who grew up in Cape Town, South Africa. She decided to leave law school and Cape Town to study at the famous Le Cordon Bleu in London. Soon after, she worked at the Marriott Hotel in South Bank, London, before returning to South Africa, where she decided to pursue her dream of becoming a food blogger.

Her website and social media accounts started out full of recipes for sugary treats, but as her lifestyle began to change due to IBS and polycystic ovary syndrome, she decided to turn the blog around and focus on creating a whole and balanced way of eating for herself and her followers. Refusing to let her health conditions define her, Zorah knew she had to make lifestyle changes. She believes moderation is key, as well as listening to your body and what it needs.

Her food has been featured on many famous sites, including @feedfeed, @feedfeedbaking, @thekitchn, @food52, @huffposttaste, @lecreuset, as well as popular magazines such as *Cosmopolitan*, *WWTaste* and *Essentials*.

Index